Rea
Kids' Stuff

Ann Baker is a freelance consultant in the fields of reading and mathematics education. She has lectured in Literacy at the Brisbane and Gold Coast Colleges of Education, and was a Research Fellow in Mathematics Education at Chelsea College, London. As co-author of the successful maths scheme, *Young Australia Maths*, she has firsthand knowledge of educational practice and problems in Australia. Most importantly, she has a wide experience of helping young children develop into confident readers — not only as a classroom teacher, but also as the mother of two adult children and pre-school twins.

Kerry Cue, a Chemistry and Maths teacher for ten years, found herself ill-equipped for parenthood, armed only with a knowledge of quadratic equations and the colour of litmus. Since then she has turned her hand to more humorous pursuits producing two children, five humorous books — including *Born to Whinge*, an unreliable guide to parenting — and numerous articles for newspapers and magazines on every topic imaginable except the colour of litmus!

Reading is Kids' Stuff

A SURVIVAL KIT FOR TODAY'S PARENTS

ANN BAKER and KERRY CUE

Collins Dove
Melbourne Australia

Published by Collins Dove
23–27 Huntingdale Road
Burwood Victoria 3125
Telephone (02) 805 1777

Developed by Eleanor Curtain Publishing
Production by Sylvana Scannapiego
Illustrated by Annie White
Designed by Sharon Carr
Typeset by Trade Graphics Pty Ltd
Printed by The Book Printer

National Library of Australia
Cataloguing-in-Publication data:

Baker, Ann

Reading Is Kids' Stuff: a survival kit for
today's parents.

ISBN 0 85924 851 8.

1.   Reading — Parent Participation. 2
     Reading (Preschool). 1. Cue, Kerry, 1952–

11. Title

     649.58

Contents

Foreword

These days parents suffer from information overload. If you try to follow half of the sensible and a quarter of the crack-pot ideas thrust upon you in the guise of 'good advice', you will be rushing your toddlers off to computer literacy courses or flashing Shakespearian sonnets at your new-born child. Some parents feel that giving their children a goal-oriented high-pressure infancy will give their children a head start in our goal-oriented high-pressure existence. And this is possibly quite right for them.

But there are those of us who believe that children learn best in a warm and loving environment. We believe that to watch children develop and grow at their own pace is as mysterious and wonderful as the unfolding of a butterfly's wings. And, like butterflies, children will take off when they are ready to go.

This book is for parents who want their children to develop at their own rate in a supportive environment. It is full of practical hints and stimulating ideas which will assist us all — parents and teachers alike — to encourage a child's reading and language development using ordinary and every-day situations. Above all, *Reading is Kids' Stuff* is not about teaching children to read, but about encouraging them to learn to read themselves, to want to learn and to enjoy the whole process.

My contribution to this book is as a parent reporting in

from the suburban front. I pick up the distress signals from various educational bunkers across the land and pass them on to Ann, whose thoughtful replies provide me with a sensible assault plan and a shot of courage for flagging spirits.

When I find myself drowning in a sea of educational jargon I call out to Ann for help and she rescues me with a simple sentence. At times I feel that Ann is expecting too much of me as a parent. But then, just when I am absorbed in the demands of everyday life and feel guilty because my 'Good Parenting' badge has been tarnished, Ann offers solace with the suggestion that children learn as long as you include them in your life.

And finally, I'm involved in this book for the fun of it. My contribution covers the humorous and ridiculous side of this learning business from answering those unanswerable questions,

'Do whales get hiccups?'

to fathoming those unfathomable answers

Q: 'You don't want any spaghetti, do you?'

A: 'No.'

After all, like children, there are times when a dose of good cheer — that's me — and encouragement — that's Ann — is all a parent wants.

Kerry Cue

Introduction

'I can read this book. Shall I read it to you?'

Prue aged 4½

Some children learn to read before they come to school. Some learn very quickly when they come to school. These children have not been taught to read at home and yet have learnt a great deal. Although this book is not specifically written to develop pre-school readers, it does look at what is special about children for whom reading came early and easily. There have been many studies into the background of young fluent readers. These studies suggest most of them came from backgrounds where reading was a family hobby, where the children were read to regularly, often from birth.

The experiences children have before they come to school influence to a very large extent their readiness for reading. Some children entering school are definitely advantaged, their language, experiences and contact with books and stories have prepared them for what lies ahead. Such children are motivated to want to learn to read and write. They know what reading is about and how print works. They know that reading can give pleasure, that books hold a wonderful world of stories. They know how reading and writing is used in real life. They have expectations of print.

Advantaged children have had many different experiences. Experiences that have contributed to their knowledge and their language development. They have heard and experienced language used for many different purposes and in many different

1

ways. They themselves have tried out many different language patterns, the patterns of rhymes, stories, instructions, directions, requests and so on. Language patterns that are like the language of teaching and the language of books. And above all such children have developed a positive view of themselves as talkers, listeners, readers and writers. Within the security of their own family or others caring for them they have shared and been part of an environment where reading, writing and talking are an everyday part of life, where everyone is successful in the task of reading and writing, where they too are expected naturally and easily to succeed.

This book is about making sure that your children are advantaged too. The focus is on creating a warm friendly setting in which talk, writing, books, play, television, magazines and the radio contribute to the development of children who are all set to read. This book does not try to show you how to teach your children to read. There are no exercises here, just ideas for natural learning situations and experiences — situations that will motivate, invite and engage children in reading. Some children will become readers as a result of such an approach. Others will be prepared and ready to read when they go to school. They will fit readily into the school's reading and writing program and be ready to benefit from it.

Basically, if we want our children to read we must entice them into the world of books. We must make it impossible for them to be able to resist the wonderful world that reading opens up. To do this we must read to our children frequently not just books, but letters, lists, newspapers, magazines, labels, signs and captions too. As we do this we are modelling what reading is, how it works and why it is so essential.

'The red hot molten lava erupted and ran down the volcano.'
Bevan 3½

If we want our children to be fluent readers we also need to extend the background of their language and experience. Play, outings, activities, talk, discussions, and books all contribute to the ever expanding world view and knowledge that children have. It is this knowledge that children use to predict and comprehend stories they hear, books they read and stories they write themselves.

For our children to succeed in reading and writing at school we also need to ensure that they are motivated and have a reasonable concentration span. Children who know what books have to offer and have listened attentively to stories will be motivated and able to concentrate. They will also have felt supported in their own developing understandings of and attempts to 'read' stories. They will be confident and willing to have a go.

Each chapter in this book explains more fully how to help your child develop what the researchers call a 'literacy set' — a view of and a readiness for literacy. Many of the chapters offer starter activities. Once you get going these will become second nature to you and you'll be generating ideas of your own as well. And don't worry, many of the suggested ideas can be carried out in those odd ten minutes here and there, at bedtime, while out in the car or shopping. Many of them can also be handed over to big brothers and sisters, grandparents and friends; in fact shared in and enjoyed by all who have your children's interests at heart.

So, get going right now:

- dip into one of the chapters, for example the television chapter, discuss it with your partner or friend;

- make this book suit your needs and answer your questions as they arise;

- write all over it, add any extra ideas to the lists, comment on how things went. You may have more children or friends who need advice and this will be helpful;

- treat this book as you would a recipe book — flip through it, choose bits that appeal to you or you feel able to attempt right now.

Of course, if you prefer, there is nothing wrong with reading it right through first.

CHAPTER 1

Yatter, Yatter, Yatter

——————— Did I Say That? ———————

When parents cross the threshold proudly holding a gurgling little bundle in their arms, they often don't realise that they are actually carrying an activated tape-recorder into the house neatly wrapped in a bunny rug. Babies are like that. They record all the household 'sayings' and 'catch phrases' from birth then start to replay them at about two years of age.

Sometimes toddlers know what they are saying and sometimes they don't. It's a learning process. But even if they don't know what they are saying, they know absolutely when to say it.

The reaction of parents to these regurgitated phrases is intriguing. Sometimes parents are delighted, excited, amused. Sometimes parents are shocked, outraged, appalled. It all depends on what the parents have said when the little tape-recorder is listening.

On the plus side parents often get back a good deal of positive encouragement in bizarre situations.

'Good Boy, Mummy' exclaimed the three-and-a-half-year-old toddler in our house as he burst in on me in the toilet.

'You are a very good boy. I wipe your bottom now.'

'No...no...no...thank you. I can do it.'

'I do it.'

'No. I'll do it thank you.'

The scene ends with mother and son grappling for control of the toilet paper.

More positive feedback came from son as a four-year-old helping Mum with a jigsaw puzzle.

'Come on Mum.' he enthused. 'You can do it. Yes you can. I know you can do it if you try.'

I vowed to be less patronising in the future.

And, of course, many of these statements are amusing. When asked to stay for dinner at a friend's house we were all amused by the three-year-old's reply 'No thank you. I have arranged to eat out this evening.'

Then there is the negative feedback. I have heard a three-year-old respond to his mother's request to wash his hands with the melodramatic reply 'Can't you wait one minute'. I have seen a three-and-a-half-year-old looking at the up-turned toy box saying 'I can't cope. I just can't cope', and a four-year-old replying to a parent's request to pick up his toys with the memorable line 'I've only got one set of hands, you know.'

And when standing firm on a 'you *will* have a bath tonight' issue, Master 6 has came out with the line 'Mum, you are excruciatingly pathethic sometimes.'

'Where did you learn that?' I asked.

'Aw. You say it all the time' he said.

I hadn't realised, though I was a touch proud of my efforts.

Then there are the swear words. I have heard flustered parents come out with this explanation more than once.

'He said 'truck'. He did. It was 'truck'. It's just that he says 'truck' with an 'f'.

And, naturally, the little tape recorder is so thrilled at the adult reponse he continues.

'Truck! Truck! Truck!' he says with an 'f'.

Learning about swearing is just learning about the rules of language. As children grow they soon learn that you don't say, 'Please don't kick me, it hurts', in the playground as it is ineffective; and you don't say 'Nick off, Nana' as that is impolite. There are rules.

This is a humungous, grizzly monster eating dead toads.'

Clare 4½

Some children learn to read before they come to school and some learn very quickly when they begin school. Researchers investigating what it is that helps this early reading development have discovered that the early readers:

o are confident language users, with a large vocabulary;
o have been encouraged to talk about their experiences, which have been varied;
o have books in the home which they have listened to frequently.

So what is a confident language user? What's so special about them?

Firstly, they are willing to express themselves. They have had many conversations, they have talked, listened and above all been listened to. From these experiences they have learnt a lot about the social graces, who it's appropriate to talk to, about what and in what type of language and tone. They know that there are conventions in language use; for example they know to call the neighbour Mr Smith even though you call him Fred, they know to call your sister Auntie Vi even though you call her Violet. They know to say excuse me when they want to interrupt an adult conversation but wouldn't dream of saying it to children when they are talking. This is the kind of knowledge that only comes from real communication and conversations with a variety of people.

Children who are confident language users are flexible language users, they are receptive and creative. They then bring all their previous language experiences to bear on the task of reading and writing. Before they start to read they will already have met most of the words and many of the sentence structures typical of children's books. This will make it possible for them to anticipate what might come next in any written sentence or story, and to recall and retell stories, to 'talk like a book' or even memorise a story, all of which are vital first steps in becoming a reader.

I always talked to her, even when she was a few days old. If I read a magazine while she was playing on my lap, I read it out loud to her. When we played with her, bathed her, or dressed her we chatted away. From a very early age she seemed to like this and joined in with gurgles. She talked very early and we encouraged her. We never used baby language and always used proper names for things. If she said 'birdie', we would add 'Yes, that bird's a magpie, lorikeet or whatever.' We also added information 'Yes, that's a red car.' We read her lots of books, of course, and talked to her about the games she played with her toys. When we had visitors we used to make sure she was part of the conversation too. Some people still think children shouldn't interrupt. We don't, we think they should be part of the whole social scene that we engage in. Some of our friends think she shouldn't be reading yet. We didn't teach her. She just sort of did it on her own. She prefers being read to though.'

This description of how Poppi learnt to talk and then read highlights the importance of talking and sharing with young children. All children's progress in talking and using language effectively will be enhanced and accelerated if they are talked to, and engaged in conversations. They will express themselves clearly and confidently. They will make themselves understood and use language to express their needs, wants and ideas.

'... but look, there is a tiny spot of blood. It's really deep. It hurts. It needs a bandaid so germs don't get in.'　　　　　Priscilla 4

Confident language users have also experienced language used creatively, descriptively, metaphorically.

'The witch is ugly and horrid. She's got a cold heart.'

Troy 4

'What's for dinner Dad?'

'Fried worms on a bed of mashed gumleaves and pureed weeds with toasted banksias spiked with wriggly grubs.'

'Delicious, can we have a cup of muddy water with slime ice-cubes to wash it down?'

This dialogue is a typical pre-dinner event in the Greene household. The ritual began when Dad was asked for the twentieth time, 'How long till dinner?' and 'What's to eat?'. Bob made up a story like the one above and invited the children to try it too. It's now a family institution and the family are always on the look out and listen for ideas to add to their repertoire, trying always to sound like the menu in a restaurant. In fact whenever they are out they look at menus in restaurant windows for more inspiration.

Listening to Bob's children and their use of descriptive and creative language explains why they are so ready to enjoy and join in with the descriptive language used in books. Descriptions of places, people and events that their language experiences allow them to visualise and embellish.

Children who are frequently talked to are developing wide vocabularies that include everyday words, special words related to special subjects, names of places, people and unusual things. Words like, 'also, especially, though, estuary, doberman, triangular, ferocious, Tokyo, Prime Minister.' Words that two, three and four-year-olds are not usually expected to understand or use. Words that many adults would not use when they talk to children. A wide vocabulary helps with reading because if children understand the words used in the text or story they will comprehend the story easily and be able to work out what an unknown word is from their understanding and familiarity with the text.

'Look! A tractor with big wheels.'

Sam 3

The language that young children use stems from the activity or objects they are engaged with, their needs (want a drink), their emotions (want a hug), or are initiated by an adult. Young children don't usually initiate a conversation for example about yesterday's trip to the park unless something reminds them of it.

Experiences and excursions also provide contexts for extending children's vocabularies and view of the world. They provide opportunities for you to reflect together on an event or experience. Children love to hear stories about themselves,

'Do you remember the day we went to the park and you made a friend called Louise. You played on the see-saw together.' Children will respond with additional information,

'We had icecream',

'I fell over and cut my knee',

and with fantasy,

'We're going to go to a fairy castle together next time!' Incidents like these have many benefits. They encourage children to:

o reflect on an event or situation;
o retell or resequence an event or situation;
o add to and embellish a story;
o create new stories.

These are all skills that readers and writers need if they are to persevere in the task. Children who have shared such conversations also have the ability to concentrate on the event or story being retold, a vital skill to beginning reading.

'Can we read "Rapunzel, Rapunzel let down your hair"?'
Priscilla 4

Early readers have also been read to a great deal. They have books in the home. To a large extent books have also contributed to their language development and vocabularies as well as to their ability to concentrate for reasonably long periods of time. The role of books in the development of children's language, concentration and thinking processes can not be ignored. Neither can talking, listening, reading and writing be separated from the total experience of being read to. Reading promotes listening which promotes talking and writing which leads to more reading and so it goes on, naturally.

In summary, books are full of words, full of ideas expressed in words, full of humour, adventure, sorrow expressed in words, full of fantasy, dreams, our worst fears all expressed in words, full of places we'll never visit, couldn't visit, people we haven't met, situations we can never experience, all brought to life by words. Of course, how the words are chosen, arranged for best effect is also a vital part of books. Reading then is largely a language process. To get the most from books we need to be confident language users, we need to have had a variety of language experiences. So:

o Set time aside to talk and listen to your children.
o Provide activities and excursions to promote language development, reasoning, thinking, reflection and story telling.
o Involve your children in adult conversations.
o Praise and respond to your children when they communicate with you (be it at the babble, one word, two word or full sentence stage).
o Do not use baby talk or deliberately restrict the vocabulary you use. Talk naturally as you normally would. If your children don't hear lots of words, they won't use or understand lots of words.
o Read and share books with your children frequently.

Activities

Take time out, right now and initiate a conversation with your children. What should you talk about? The options are infinite:

- what your children are doing/playing;

- something your children have shown an interest in in the last hour, day, week;

Or, if it's very quiet around your house, do something right now that will generate conversation:

- Have a teddy's tea party (teddys can talk you know).

- Go for a walk (play 'What can you see.' 'I can see an enormous tree with no leaves.').

- Make finger puppets of ghosts or princes from paper and act out little scenes or stories.

- Polish the sink together (make it gleam, glitter, glow).

Or if you prefer it quiet, reflect on something you have done together in the past:

- A trip to the fish market ('Do you remember the smelly fish market. You held your nose and said pooh pooh pooh' ...)

Use language creatively, expressively, vividly:

- Tell tall stories, exaggerated stories about everyday events, objects, people. Turn the everyday into an adventure or mystery.

- Make up stories that include your children and their friends.

- Retell favourite stories from your childhood, about you or your children. Children love to hear about what you or they were like when they were small.

- Sing songs, chants, jingles together.

Provide unusual situations or materials for your children to describe and explore:

- Provide a variety of smells/tastes for the children to describe, introducing words like, rancid, foetid, fishy, lemony, tart, sweet, salty.

- Make an egg head. After the boiled egg is eaten up, cotton wool can be pushed into the shell, a face drawn on it and cress sown on the cotton wool. After a few days, egg head will have hair.

And remember, listen to your children and value their contributions.

CHAPTER 2

What Can Children Learn About Reading Before They Come to School

Survival Reading

Children learn early on that parents react most remarkably to those things called signs. And signs aren't things you just read. They are things you shout about.

'That sign says DON'T TOUCH'

'It says DON'T WALK'

'That signs says DON'T...DON'T...'

'WET PAINT...And don't touch me until I get a tissue.' Children realise quickly that being able to read signs is a matter of SURVIVAL. It is SURVIVAL READING.

'Quick. Quick. Which one is for girls? I can't tell.' And, of course, it is very hard to read anything when you are hopping around on one foot just about to wet your pants.

But soon they can read toilets, and toilets come in all sorts of different signs. There are BOY and GIRL toilets. MEN and WOMEN toilets. LADIES and GENTLEMEN toilets (or for places that save on paint, LADIES and GENTS). Girl in a dress and boy not in a dress toilets. Very quickly children learn to read them all.

Children learn to read all sorts of signs as they discover their value. Thus they start to read shop signs at a very early age.

'I want to go to K-Mart.'

'There's Reddy Red Rooster!'

'Can we have a Pizza tonight?'

Then there are the signs in shops.

'I want a Bubble-o-Bill.'

'A what?'

'A Bubble-o-Bill. Look. Up there. The one with the bubble gum on his nose.'

I'm amazed that children can make sense out of the clutter of signs in the Milk Bar. I stand, gazing at the ice cream signs rather starstruck. Yet children can pick the ice cream they want — the most expensive — they can tell you the latest addition to the range, they can tell you its name and where to locate it in the freezer.

Then there are the brand names. The problem is, once children can identify brand names you are in for big money. No more being fobbed off with cheap imitations.

'I want a real Dribbling Doris Doll for my birthday.'

'I want a genuine remote controlled Smasher Basheroo Truck for Christmas.'

'Look. They've got Chuppapoozels with the real bbq taste.'

'Can I have a Wonga Bar that really satisfies that hungry feeling?'

And so on.

Then finally there are road signs.

'Kerry, doesn't that sign say KEEP LEFT?' asked my son's seven-year-old-mate as we stopped at the intersection.

'Yes it does.'

We all looked at the sign. We were to the right of the sign.

'Ah, that's interesting,' I said, quickly reversing the car and pulling up to the left of the sign.

'Now we're alright. We're left.'

I tried to exude an aura of confidence, but the two seven-year-old males read traffic signs at me for the rest of the trip. But at least they had discovered SURVIVAL reading.'

'I know what this sign says. It says N-O- Sm-ok-ing'
Edward 3½

It actually said 'No Smoking in these toilets'. But Edward matched what he thought the sign was saying to what he 'read' as his pointing finger moved across the sign. But never mind. It showed that he had learned a lot about print. For example he knew, that:

o signs convey a message;
o red on white might well be NO SMOKING;
o print goes from left to right;
o he has a language model for signs, that is that they are short and to the point;
o print always says the same thing, it does not change.

Current research into how children learn about print suggests that they begin to attend to signs quite early in life. They recognise that signs carry a message and later what that message is. Later still they begin to focus on elements within the sign like the first letter of words.

'Exit looks like Emma'   Richard

Often the information recognised is highly personal. Richard had begun to recognise the first letter of his friend's names on the labels at pre-school. One day while out shopping he pointed to the exit sign, named it and then related the way it began to the way his friend Emma's name began.

'TOILET has two Ts'   Richard

14

On the same shopping trip Richard noticed that TOILET began and ended with a T. This was a source of much fascination and began a search for other words that began and ended with the same letter. Richard in these two examples demonstrated that:

o he recognises some words;
o recognises some letters;
o realises that words are made up by a group of letters;
o expects there to be some pattern in spelling;
o realises that many words can begin with the same letter.

If interpreting a sign involves such a wide range of knowledge and experiences what does reading captions or books involve? Children who sit on a lap having stories read to them on a regular basis learn that:

o Print carries the message. The pictures add to that message.
o Print can give pleasure and satisfaction in a very special way.
o A book has a cover, pages, a front, a back, a spine.
o A book is read from front to back.
o Print runs from left to right, top to bottom.
o Books have different language patterns.
o Books make sense, they tell stories or recount events in a very stylised way.
o They can predict what might happen next in a story.
o They can retell or recount the story.

You didn't read it properly. You didn't say 'I'll huff and I'll puff.'
Troy 3 ½

Children who come to school with a limited experience of print and books do not have this headstart. For them, some time at school will be spent developing these understandings. At this same time other children will be becoming readers. The point here is that without actually teaching your children you can be preparing them for reading.

As your children sit on your lap to listen to a story or look at a magazine, you are passing on in the most natural way positive attitudes, curiosity, values, and skills. For example, as you read *The Hungry Caterpillar* by Eric Carle you are snuggled up together feeling relaxed and cosy. There are important messages here for your children. They feel relaxed and warm towards the book. They see that you value reading and books. They see that reading is worthwhile, purposeful and above all enjoyable.

As the story unfolds they will be curious about what the caterpillar will eat next and what will happen to him. They will be expecting answers to their questions. They will be expecting the story to have a happy outcome. This curiosity and expectation will be extended to other books that you share and later to books the children read themselves. This is the basis for comprehension. The children expect print to make sense, therefore when they begin to read they will expect their reading to make sense. The expression and intonation you use as you read will add to this comprehension and will encourage your children to read expressively too.

At the close of the story your children will have learnt a lot about the life cycle of the caterpillar. Their values may have changed too. They will see caterpillars and butterflies in a new light. They will begin to understand how exciting the life cycle is and how wonderful nature is. They will have sat still and concentrated on the story, listening carefully as they do so. As you share more and longer stories with your children so their concentration span will grow. This is an essential attribute for many school tasks and especially for reading.

And if that is not enough they will also have learnt or added to their understanding of what print is and how it works. They may have noticed for example how the pictures help to predict the text, 'On Tuesday he ate through...' and there is the picture to provide the answer. Some children will join in perhaps noticing where it says 'On Tuesday'.

In short, everytime you share print with your children you will be passing on very important messages and skills.
In summary:

o Children need many experiences with print of all types before they come to school.

- ○ Children begin to attend to print and signs very early in life.
- ○ Children who have been read to develop many ideas about what print is and how it works before they come to school.
- ○ Don't teach your children, just involve them in a variety of print activities.
- ○ Make reading a happy, relaxed time.
- ○ Through children's language, experiences and comprehension are developed and extended.

Activities

Start right now. Help your children value reading, develop a positive attitude to reading and begin to unlock print. For example you could:

- Read a book, read it as many times as your children like.

- Invite your children to respond to a book, drawing a character from the book, making playdough models, making simple finger puppets out of paper, retelling parts of the story. Use the story as the basis of games and play.

- Invite your children to help you cook, they can collect the ingredients as you point to them in the recipe and carry out some of the pouring and mixing as you read out the instructions.

- Read out the instructions from the manual or box as you set the video, try out your new vacuum, assemble a new toy or use a new bubble bath.

- Make a book together, using photos of your children and write about them. Let your children illustrate and dictate or write their own stories. Add captions to your children's pictures. These will become favourite reading material.

When you open up the wonderful world of print for your children, keep it warm and friendly and let your children set the pace.

CHAPTER 3

Writing is Important Too

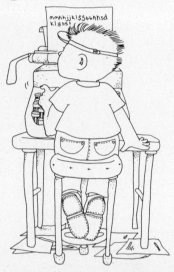

——— Words, the Universe and Everything ———

Once children realise that we speak words, we write words and we read words, the universe is theirs. For words are the spaceships we build around us to blast us into another dimension. Words are the arrows which we can prime with enthusiasm to fire ideas at other people. Words are the gossamer fine threads of human thought that tie the past to the present, the present to the future.

Words are the mysteries, the adventures, the sorrow and the striving of human kind trapped within the dog-eared pages of the favourite book. Words are more brilliant than the summer sun, sweeter than the sweetest honey, more frightening than the most shrill cry at night and more brutal than a pin piercing an eye. Children begin to tell us who they are with words. They tell us their hopes and fears. And there are lots and lots of words to choose from.

'What have I written?' asked Master 4 after bashing away

at the typewriter.

'You've written mmmmhhjjkl$$$6666hhhhssssdjklus ssstttt5...'

'Oh'

'What did you want to write?'

'I wanted to write 'This here is Julian's typewriter''. Ah, yes. The possessive word.

'Mum. How do you spell HOORAH?'

Now that's the Happy-and-you-know-it word.

Door Sign: 'No gild alowd in this rom'.

The BOSSY word.

Jar sign: 'Danjr pioson'

The warning word.

Shopping list sign on cupboard: 'Buy more choccolot bas'

The hungry word.

Card: 'I luv my mummy and my daddy luv Jenni'

The loving word.

Chalk on pavement: 'Pis Off from Adrian'.

The rude word.

Work Sheet; 'Mum it says 'Very Good Work'.

The encouraging word.

Painting of Icecream falling; 'PLOP. PLOP. PLOP'

The funny word.

'FLASH GORDON IV.R.I.P.'

The sad word.

Word on trick box: SHAZAM

The magic word.

Words can do anything. We can contain the universe in the palm of our hand if we can read words. But if we can write words we can go one step further, we can let the universe know that we are here!

'That's not writing, that's scribble'

Mum is in the bank filling out slips. Frankie is filling out slips too. Frankie says to Mum, 'I'm writing too', and looks disappointed at her reply. Mum can be forgiven for thinking that Frankie was simply scribbling. But let's look closely at what Frankie was actually doing. She had:

o created squiggles just like her Mum's;
o written from left to right across the page, just like Mum;
o tried to create a message, just like Mum.

Had she been asked to, Frankie could no doubt have 'read' her message to us. She was imitating her mother's behaviour. She was using writing as part of her role play. She created a message and a way of expressing it, and as such, her efforts were worthy of praise, not criticism. Given encouragement and opportunity to see writing in progress, children soon invent and create their own shopping lists, letters, messages and stories. And as they do so, some real letters begin to find their way into the strings of scribble.

When your baby babbled at you, like most other parents you probably smiled and talked back. 'That's a clever girl. Tell me all about it.' In so doing you let your baby know that you valued the attempted communication. You knew that this was the first step along the road to real talk.

Fig. 1

In the same way when your children scribble (Figure 1) they are making their first step along the road to writing. Babbling if you like is scribble talk. Scribble is its equivalent. And just as your baby moved from babble to recognisable sounds so too your child will move from scribble to recognisable writing.

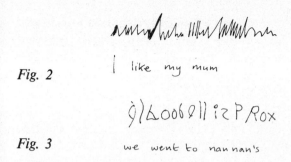

Fig. 2

Fig. 3

Figures 2 and 3 show the first steps from scribble to something that is recognisable as writing. In Figure 2 we see that directionality is being developed as the string of imitation writing proceeds from left to right across the page. Then in Figure 3 some recognisable letters are included. Examples like these are, like babble and daddas, worthy of recognition and praise. Just as you expect baby's babble to move closer and closer towards real talk so too you should expect scribble writing to move closer and closer towards real writing and real spelling. And just as you valued each new step along the road to talking, making an effort to understand what was said, supporting and extending naturally and spontaneously each attempt, so too similar attempts at writing and spelling should be supported. If children see that you value their attempts at writing and take them seriously they will feel confident to make other attempts. They will perceive themselves as writers and continue to write and experiment with written forms. If however they receive negative feedback or little feedback at all in response to their efforts they may feel discouraged.

There are recognisable stages in children's development of language. Similar stages exist in the development of children's writing and spelling. The same understanding, support and acceptance that existed for learning language also need to exist for children to learn writing. So let's look at the parallels between learning to talk and learning to write.

As children learn to talk they take risks, try things out. At first babies hear talk as strings of noises. They make a noise too. Soon they begin to distinguish recognisable sounds. They try to make those sounds too. Soon they learn that words relate to objects. They try to use those words as labels too. If you look at the children's scribble in Figures 1, 2 and 3 you can see this same progression there. At first a general scribble, then scribble that shows some understanding of what writing is and then some real letters included.

Fig. 4

I P Wi mi CAt
I played with my cat

In Figure 4 we see how letters have been used to stand for words as the writing begins to more closely resemble 'real' writing.

How do children make these moves towards writing? They practise and gain confidence, they will look at print to find out how it works. They will watch you as you write. They will ask,

'What's that letter?'

'What's that word?'

'Does that say hello?'

'There's my name isn't it?'

'What's that squiggle?'

As they watch you and talk to you about what you are doing they will be learning about writing. They will be learning what's a letter and what's a word. They will attend to:

o conventions of print such as spaces between words and punctuation, e.g. question marks, full stops;
o how a letter, shopping list, form is set out;
o what kind of language and language structure is used in each instance.

Not only does this help with their writing it also helps with their reading. Similarly as they read, or are read to, they will be developing other understandings of writing. Understandings that will be displayed in their writing attempts.

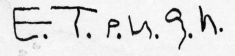

Edward 4

In this example, what looks like a string of letters was read by Edward, 'E.T. phone home', as he pointed to the letters. Noticing that he hadn't pointed to the G he was asked what the G was for. The response 'because sometimes E.T. says go home', demonstrated how inventive young children can be and also highlights the developmental stage reached. Although Edward had some idea about the sequential nature of writing, left to right, one letter for each word, he still has a way to go. For example inserting alternative information (G for go) in the middle of a sentence is not a normal writing convention.

Children need to see many examples of writing and experience many writing purposes to help them make the move towards writing. Just as a baby is talked to, involved in family conversations, hears the radio, is sung songs, told nursery rhymes, so a beginner writer needs the same variety of experiences.

Children talking and telling stories as they draw are in a sense writing. Listen to the stories and ask questions, give comments, and if invited write the stories for the children, so demonstrating the writing process.

Let your children set the pace just as they did when they learnt to talk. They'll know when they want to 'write', what they want to 'write' about, and how long they'll want to spend on the activity. Follow along and facilitate. Expect the children to develop ideas about writing over time. Don't push for instant conformity.

In summary:

o value each attempt at writing;
o respond positively;
o read or ask your children to 'read' what they've written;
o comment positively on the story, asking questions or naturally adding to it;
o provide plenty of opportunities for them to observe you writing;
o involve them in deciding what to write about, or how to express something for best effect.

Activities

Now is as good a time as any other to get started, so why not ask your children to:

- help you write the shopping list or better still write their own lists at the same time as you;

- sign their names on a card or letter;

- draw a picture, write a story, birthday request or letter to one of their favourite television shows;

- write your children's stories as they tell them to you and together read them back;

- write and draw their own stories;

- make labels for their rooms, toy boxes etc;

- cut out words from magazines to make messages, captions or stories;

- cut out faces from magazines and make up thought or speech bubbles for them

- collect forms from the bank, post office etc. so that your children can fill them in (like Frankie did in the bank).

There are many accessories that can add to this list and encourage more writing activities such as coloured pens, letter templates, dymo labellers, labels, an old typewriter, magnetic letters and name or letter puzzles.

Remember to value each attempt, even if you can't read it. With time and effort, you will be able to interpret some of your children's writing, just as you were once able to interpret their babble. And you can always say: 'Read me your story.'

Your children will be able to tell you what it says.

CHAPTER 4

We're All Different You Know

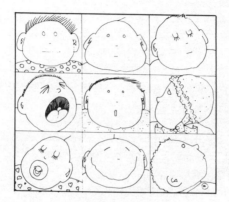

—— When I grow up I'm going to be Myself ——

The good thing about being a grown-up is that you can be yourself. No one is running around with a chart saying 'I'm really worried about your development. Look, at 35 years of age you should be able to read financial magazines, tune a Volvo, do tax returns, cook *coq-au-vin*, run a marathon, wallpaper a toilet and windsurf.' It would be abysmal trying to keep up with the expectations of others for all of our lives. Fortunately, we do accept diversity of talents in adults.

Yet, when psychologists elbowed their way into childhood they hammered away and set up rigid guidelines for child development covering such milestones as when a child should smile, wink, hop and think.

The problem with all of this is that guidelines produce expectations and expectations produce pressure. We live in

Reading is Kids' Stuff

the age of informed parenting and we have a lot more to worry about. First-time parents are especially vulnerable to coaching their children in the art of talking, walking, pooing or chewing to keep up with the child-rearing textbook.

The irony is, many adults would not live up to the rigid development guidelines applied to children.

Take smiling for instance. Some psychologists expect babies to smile at around six weeks of age. I like that. Here is a group of professionals who look as if they have never smiled in their lives, telling parents when a child should smile. If it doesn't smile at six weeks the parents should be happy. Their child is obviously going to grow up to be a psychologist.

Now let's consider hopping. Some States use 'hopping' in their school readiness tests. Hopping! Good heavens. If you took groups of merchant bankers and said 'Alright. Hop or you're out of the bank', I think we'd soon be running out of merchant bankers.

I have often wondered why our expectations are so high for children, when we are willing to make so many exceptions for adults.

As a parent it is difficult not to have some expectations for our children. But I don't wish to drag my children down some clearly marked pathway of life. Rather, I hope, I can stand with them and show them the open road saying, 'I can't promise you anything on this road to life, except one thing — it's going to be a GREAT ADVENTURE.'

'Jane can write her name now', boasted Marg.
'Oh, John can't even recognise his', worried Robin.

Have you noticed how unalike individuals in some families are. You wonder how 'the joker' or 'the pessimist' ever came to be part of the same family. Well, all kids are different. Every child is unique. That means that comparisons between what little Johnny can do and what little Jane can do are pointless. Kids grow at different rates. We don't worry about that. Kids want to do or learn different things at different rates and if they seem slow we may panic or if they seem bright we may think we have a genius on our hands. It is natural for children to develop at different rates, to have different interests and things that preoccupy them at different stages.

This can be clearly seen if you consider the range of interests and talents within your family or circle of friends. The chances are that you know someone who was not very academic at school but developed academically later in life; perhaps even went back to school or college as a mature student. Maybe you know someone who failed school and went on to become a millionaire or business magnate. It happens. You probably know people who are artistic, musical, mathematical, scientific, practical, mechanical or good at language. You accept this as natural. So accept your children's strengths and weaknesses. You no doubt also know people who are active, passive, quiet, loud, funny, serious, talkative or withdrawn. You accept them for what they are. They have characteristics or traits that attract you to them or that you admire. So do your children. Just stop worrying or flapping and relax.

Children then have different interests, strengths and personalities that may well influence the way and the rate at which they learn.

'I don't want to listen to a story.'   Martin

Martin hated story books. He always did. He liked cold hard facts, dinosaurs, fossils, animals, space, motors. Careful selection of books that also provided information made it possible to introduce Martin to story books. Books like, *Gumdrop, There's a Dinosaur in the Park, The Chameleon*, broadened his horizons. Slowly he became more tolerant of fiction. This became evident in his play and later selection of books at the library. This was a relief to his parents who feared that he would not want to read at school where books for the early years are mainly fiction.

By listening to his interests, accepting his preferences and tailoring the choice of books to his needs his parents were able

to prepare him for the world of books and school.
Parents or care-givers can support children's individuality by:

o accepting their differences;
o emphasising their strengths;
o expecting success;
o choosing and providing experiences that support and extend
  personal interests;
and above all
o by staying calm.

A preschool teacher had a little boy called David in her class.
He spoke beautifully and could read as well as any eleven-year-
old. The teacher worried about what she could do to stretch
him. And then she noticed that his manipulative skills were
extremely underdeveloped. He couldn't stack the blocks, he
couldn't draw or cut at all, his approach to most activities was
very uncoordinated. When she spoke to his parents, they agreed
and said they'd always concentrated on language activities with
him because he always enjoyed them the most. Talking to David
they discovered that there were other things he now wanted
to learn: he wanted to catch and throw a ball and he wanted
to draw pictures. He wasn't a genius, but a child who had
developed one aspect of his ability. Kids often do this. They
concentrate on things they like doing, or things that they know
please other people. In that way they develop strengths at the
expense of other areas which may then become weaknesses.

David's parents gave him the confidence he needed to pursue his language strength. They then realised that he needed
support in his weaker areas too; the support and safety that
a family can offer, safe from any fear of failure or
competitiveness.

Children not only learn at different rates they also learn
differently. Some children seem able to take little bits of
information and piece them together to make a whole. Others
seem to be able to start with the whole and break it into little
pieces. For example, some children after learning letters and
letter names or sounds are able to piece this information together

to read. For others this task is very difficult. Some children can learn to read a few sentences or words and then begin to extract letter names, sounds and rules. Some children work both ways with equal ease. There again, some children are very visual and have a strong visual memory, others are very aural and have strong aural memories (recalling rhyme, rhythm, sound, patterns very easily).

By listening to and watching children as they respond to activities and experiences we can tune in to a child's natural strengths. Activities can be tailored to fit the individual child's needs and to support and extend their own learning strengths. For example, if you often read stories to your children you are employing their visual strengths as they look at the pictures. If you involve finger puppets to add to a story-telling or reading you are again stimulating the visual aspect. On the other hand, story-telling with no props, singing songs, chanting and saying rhymes are aural activities that stimulate listening abilities. So have a mix.

Similarly if you have children who like numbers, allow time as you read stories for your children to count various objects on the page, e.g. the swarm of bees or flowers on the tree in *Goodnight Owl*. There are more ideas in the activities section.

A child who experiences failure becomes a failure.

If you are over-anxious about your children's development, or too competitive about their skills, you could be conveying messages to your children that will hamper their development. Children are perceptive and will notice if you are anxious or disappointed. This will make them anxious too as they perceive themselves as failures. When you know you've already failed, before you even begin to learn to read, where is the point in continuing to try? Similarly children who are constantly being compared to others are under pressure to achieve. If they don't achieve well enough or fast enough they too are failures. Learning to read should be stress free, so

o remember your children are unique

o   accept that your children will learn at their own rates
o   accept that development can be uneven. When you are trying really hard to develop one skill it is almost impossible to attend to another skill at the same time
o   value and acknowledge what your children can do
o   provide a broad range of activities
and above all
o   don't panic or get anxious. Anxiety is contagious

So start right now. Build on your children's interests and strengths. Provide a wide range of multi-media activities so that your children have artistic, scientific, musical, spatial experiences to build on and broaden their horizons. You never know, you may both discover you have hidden talents.

Activities

The activities that follow cater for a wide range of learning and thinking styles.

Messy Activities

- Paint for finger painting, printing, spattering, combing, dripping or just plain painting. Encourage your children to talk about and describe what they are doing and what their pictures look like or how they make them feel.

- Display the paintings or make a book of them including your children's captions or stories.

- Playdough, plasticine, clay for rolling, stretching, pulling, squidging, squashing and modelling. Enjoy the feel and the words as you squelch, squidge, squash.

- Bake models for permanence. These can be painted, displayed and captioned.

- Why not help your children make name plaques for their doors?

- Junk modelling. Boxes and junk can be sorted, compared by

size and made into fantasy models. Encourage your children to talk about what they are doing and to make up stories about their models.

- Woodwork, cooking, gardening and so on come into this category too, so make the most of them as well.

Musical Activities

- Sing songs, jingles, songs from your childhood, from playschool, from television advertisements.

- Accompany your songs with saucepan lids, home made shakers (a soft drink bottle full of rice, beans etc.) wooden spoons.

- Clap, stamp, shake, dance to the rhythm of songs you sing, songs on television, the radio or nursery cassettes.

- Recite and chant rhymes and rhythms.

- Listen to some 'great music' together and talk about how it makes you feel, what you see or imagine as you listen, memories it evokes.

- If you have rhyme or song cassettes with matching books use the two together sometimes, tying in the visual and sound images.

- Paint or 'move' to the music.

Scientific Activities

- Cook together, noticing the changes in texture (wet, dry, stiff, soft, creamy) and talking about temperature (melting, hot, cold, icy, boiling).

- Go on a nature walk, collect objects as you fossick, and bring them home to find out more about them. Sort, classify, compare and describe the objects you found on the walk.

- Maintain and oil the trike together talking about metal, plastic, animal (leather) materials used to make things.

Spatial Activities

- Make an obstacle course in the yard. Use buckets, brooms, old sheets, barrels to make things to go through, under, over, around.

- Go to the park, play on the swings, slides, roundabouts.

- Play hide and seek or hunt the thimble.

- Play blind man's buff.

- Make a beam balance for balancing using a plank across two chairs or simply some thick rope on the ground.

- Play ball games and chasing games.

Whatever the activity congratulate your children on their success. Foster their individuality. Maintain their enthusiasm. And if your children are, for example, 'clumsy', plan more activities to develop body control and spatial awareness. Tie it in with something they are good at, e.g. if language is the strong point act out stories like *Rosie's Walk, Bears in the Night.* Be creative and supportive, involve as many senses and abilities as you can.

Your Child Wants to Learn Now

'Do Whales Get Hiccups?'

Let us consider a child's curiosity.

First of all their timing is always completely and utterly off. You, the parent, will be up to your elbows in scone dough, while answering the phone — held in place by your left shoulder and neck — while using one free foot to keep the toddler out of the cat's food dish when a child, who has previously shown no interest whatsoever in the art of calligraphy, bounds in the door and demands 'HOW DO YOU WRITE ZOO?'

You, the parent, motivated by concern immediately attempts to write 'Z-O-O' in the air with your elbow. (This is quite manageable for ZOO, but totally out of the question for ornithorhynchus.)

And so it goes. You are asked 'How do you sex mice?' under the shower, (difficult at the best of times, but almost impossible under water), 'How do you turn the front hose off?' while you are in the toilet, and 'What are those really, really fat black spiders with those really, really hairy legs called?' while you are driving the car. If the timing is not enough to throw a parent into a complete wheel spin, then often the question finishes them off. For some reason the questions often asked by children are totally obscure and utterly unanswerable.

'Why are oranges round?'

'Can dogs whistle?'

'Do dingoes get headaches?'

'Do fish wee in the sea?'

'Do whales get the hiccups?'

After pondering on these matters all I can say is there are many unsolved mysteries in this world and they are all small children.

For the fiftieth time I don't know so go and ask your Dad.

Have you noticed how compulsive children can become when they get an idea into their heads? They won't even stop to eat and sometimes even forget to go to the toilet. It seems that when kids want or need to know something they have a driving force that's invincible. Why don't they concentrate at other times?

This compulsion doesn't just develop. It's there from birth. Even very young babies scream for cuddles, rocks and coos. And as they grow they have a strong compulsion to explore. Anything they get their hands on goes straight to the mouth to be investigated. The urge to become mobile to broaden the range of items to be explored follows. Babies spend hours on hands and knees trying to make that first move forward. They gurgle and babble for hours too to learn how to talk. Practice, trial and error and sheer determination move babies, toddlers and children ever closer to the models of the older people around them. And as they explore, move around, look and listen they are learning. They are probably learning faster in these first few years than they ever will again. There is an urgency and a real need to find out, a natural drive to make sense of the world.

Many two-year-olds who throw tantrums are really expressing a need or desire to know or do something now. Some at least of these confrontations with toddlers could be avoided if we:

o had the time to wait for them to explore a plant, wander the aisles of the supermarket, answer all their questions, play with them for an hour in the bath;
o had the energy to swing them again;
o didn't worry that they'd catch pneumonia while running around naked;
o understood exactly what they wanted us to do and why.

Children are not stubborn, naughty, obstinate, messy or terribly slow just to annoy us. Usually they are involved in something or wanting to do something that they have an urgent need to master or understand. This urgency for exploration and knowledge goes on for many years too. During this time the rate of learning is rapid. We can help children in this learning process and development by avoiding confrontations and understanding and supporting the children as they investigate. Often the amount of time spent pursuing one avenue of exploration is frustrating to us as adults. We have other things to do as well as wait for our offspring to touch, feel, smell, shake, taste and observe objects that interest them. We have timelines and schedules to stick to. Somehow however there needs to be space for some of both. Give and take on both sides.

Vanessa had been given an old typewriter that morning. She found the 'S' key after much scanning of the keyboard. She'd just seen 'S' and the snake on Sesame Street and was determined to find it on the keyboard. She typed a row of Ss. 'That says 'sssssss...' as she pointed along the row. 'Yes', said Dad, 'now come and get your lunch.' She ignored him and filled the whole page with Ss.

'This says 'ssssss sssss.......it's a snake.'

Dad was getting impatient. He wanted his lunch. But no, Vanessa had found another key that interested her. 'What's this one say?' she asked. Dad grudgingly said 'f.'

A new sheet of paper was demanded and Vanessa was away. A row of fs later, and she yelled, 'That says ffffff.'

'I know,' said Dad who could hardly keep a straight face. He left Vanessa to her typing. Dad had a quiet, solitary lunch. Vanessa had none. She was far too busy learning.

There's a moral to this story, which is that when we want to teach children something they often don't want to learn or at least don't seem to. And when we want lunch or a quiet cup of tea that's the very moment that they demand help with their learning.

When a child asks, 'What's this letter say?' 'Read me a book now'. 'How do you write my name?' 'What's this funny mark?' they need that information or that input right then. If you come back to them later, they won't want to know. The moment of need has passed.

When a child wants to learn and asks for help or attention, what message do they get when you say 'Not now dear', or 'I'm too busy at the moment.' What are you saying? That the child's need is minor and second to yours? That you are doing 'real' work and that what they are doing is just play? That their need to learn is not important? Sometimes your need may be able to wait but not the child's urgent need to know. So remember that your children learn best when they want to, not when you want them to, so:

o foster and support your children's desire to know, explore and understand the world;
o try not to be frustrated by your children's slow and tedious explorations;
o try to make time when your children want it;
o build on the things your children want to know;
o answer and attend to your children's questions;
o keep this drive and hunger for knowledge and understanding alive.

Activities

Find ways to broaden the range of explorations available for your children, start right now.

- Give your children new touch sensations — jelly in a polythene bag, jelly on a plate, ice-cubes.

- Take half an hour to just stroll at your children's pace talking about, looking at, smelling, feeling, listening to things that take your children's ear or eye.

- Try some new taste sensations like, chicken and chocolate, weetbix and apricot jam. Your children will have some good ideas. Inspired by Dr Seuss's *Green Eggs and Ham*, you could actually make green eggs and ham.

- Add food colouring to the bath water, yellow at one end and blue at the other.

- Let your children wash up, pour water, fill and empty cups, make bubbles.

- Make noises with rubber bands on a tissue box, rubbing a finger on a balloon, banging on bottles with different amounts of water in each.

- Draw on balloons and see what happens to them when the balloon is inflated.

Only pursue activities like these for as long as your children are interested. Follow your children's leads. They may want to do something completely different in response to each activity. And don't panic if you don't have much time, many of these activities can fit into the busiest routine. All children need a daily bath, so bath salts, colouring and bubble blowing, filling and emptying containers, pouring and straining can be part of that routine. Remember, you can provide many ideas of your own to help your children explore the world. You might enjoy re-discovering some of these things too.

CHAPTER 6

Children are Natural Learners

Beware, Teacher at Large

You can tell those parents who are teachers. You see them in art galleries, at scenic lookouts, in museums, pointing and delivering a loud dissertation to a group of uninspired offspring on the influence of seventeenth century lava flows on the artistic development of Boxer Revolution buttonholes. Teachers are like that.

Once you have taught any subject for a number of years you shift into automatic teacher and you can't stop. You see lessons behind every door, in every book, under every rock.

I've been suffering from unrestrained outbursts of teaching for years. But my children have helped me a lot.

'Mum, what does it say on this box?'

'Oh! This is interesting. Did you know this juice has vitamin C in it? And in the olden days pirates' teeth used to fall out because they didn't get vitamin C?'

'Mum, what does it say?'

'And Captain Cook knew this — sort of — and took on fresh fruit when he could. And scientists believe...'

'Mum. What does it say?'

'It says 'Open other end.''

'Thanks. I'm starving of thirst.'

I do my best. I can't help it if an extraordinary amount of worthy information keeps leaping into my conscious thoughts and popping out my mouth. My children are patient. They nod their heads and occasionally grunt.

But when they need to know something really, really interesting like 'Why do blood clots slither down your throat when you get a blood nose?' or 'How many colours are their in hundreds and thousands?' they just hammer me with questions and I don't even need a soap box. But I could do with a good reference on hundreds and thousands.

'Where's rain come from'   Andra 3

Children are natural learners. They learn despite our best attempts to teach them. They are learning all the time, especially things you don't want them to. You can't stop them learning.

Richard: *'You are not allowed to say Oh God at Preschool'*
Rene: *'You're not allowed to say damn either'*

They ask questions non stop. They ask for things to be said over and over again. They make mistakes then sort them out. They listen and observe.

Children, as we saw in the last chapter, are born with a need to know, a desire to learn, a natural curiosity. The experiences they have and the support they receive from their parents as they explore cause and effect, solve problems, seek information and extend their understandings are crucial in their development. We cannot stop children learning. We can however play a crucial role in their learning process.

We can share things with our children, involve them in things that we do and see as important. We can answer their questions, restate or retell something a number of times on request. We can stop trying to teach and just let our children learn. They will make many of the leads. They will ask questions. They will explore the whys and wherefores. 'How, why, because, if, when, where' bubble from their lips quite naturally and spontaneously. Each new activity, outing, book, poem or song will generate more questions. Even abstract ideas and strange little worries and thoughts tumble out.

'When you are old and die, I'll be big enough to drive this car, won't I Dad?'   Edward 4

The activities suggested in Chapters 4 and 5 will provide fuel for questions and natural rapid learning. So too will the sharing of songs, poems, rhymes and books. As you read to your children they listen to the words, the tone, the story. They observe the way you read from left to right across the page, the way you start at the front of the book and turn the pages, that the book always tells the same story in the same words.

Then they ask questions, why...how...when...Then they want it read again and again. Then they try to read the book themselves, retelling it, missing out a bit and having to go back, telling it in the wrong order and having to re-sequence.

As they become more comfortable with books they want to know,

'Where does it say "giant"?'

'Is this word the same as that?'

'Why can't I see an "s" on this page?'

They start to parrot the book word for word, or anticipate the story word for word as you read, and soon they actually recognise some of the words. They are learning naturally, at their own rate, in their own way. They're having fun as they do it too.

Richard picked up *The Very Hungry Caterpillar*, opened it at the first page and began to read, 'A little egg lay on a little leaf and out popped a very hungry caterpillar.' His familiarity with the story had allowed him to summarise several pages as he looked at page one. As he turned to the next page he realised that he had already 'read' it. At first he didn't know what to do. He looked puzzled and then turned back to the first page, 'read' only what was appropriate and then continued to the second page, 'reading' what was shown there. On completion of the story he asked, 'Did I read it nicely Mummy?' What could she say? That that wasn't reading only retelling? That the words on the page were not the words he'd read? And if she said 'No', would he ever want to read a book again? What she actually said was, 'Yes you really read that very nicely Richard.'

And in many ways it was well read. Although he didn't 'read' the story word for word, he showed that he knew that the story was written in a particular style, and should always be 'read' in that style. He showed that he knew the conventions of that story, that is he knew it wasn't a 'Once upon a time...' or 'A long time ago...' type of story. He demonstrated that he knew each page should tell its own part of the story. From the tone of his voice, he showed that he was enjoying the story and knew how to emphasise parts of it for effect. He also showed that he was already thinking confidently about himself as a reader. So although he didn't actually 'read' the book he demonstrated quite clearly how much he had learnt about reading. There had been no attempt to teach him to read but he had been listened to, and appreciated when it was important to him. He was learning naturally and at his own pace what reading is and how it works.

As you write your children are observing how you form letters, leave spaces between words, set out the page differently when you write a list or letter or message. They'll ask questions, 'Which bit says Aunty Vi?' 'Where are the hugs and kisses?' They'll be adding to what they already know about words and reading. But you won't have taught them a thing. They'll have learnt what is important and meaningful to them, by themselves almost.

This is the same natural learning that enabled your children to learn to talk. You didn't set out to teach them words or grammar and yet they learned that and much more besides. They learned about how language is used differently in different situations. They learned about how tone, intonation and gesture could add to speech. They learned to say things they'd never ever even heard said. They did it all naturally. Your children can make great inroads into reading, writing and spelling naturally too. Don't teach them, just let them learn. Believe it; children are natural learners. They actually want to learn. That is, until lack of response, constant negative put downs or lack of interest quells that natural curiosity. So:

o let your children decide what they want to learn from a situation;
o read to and with your children;
o follow their leads;
o let your children see you write;
o involve your children in lots of everyday reading and writing activities;
o have fun.

Activities

Start right now:

● Read some stories to your children.

● Listen to your children's responses to the stories and follow them up now while the interest is there. This may mean answering questions, talking about feelings, cooking gingerbread men, planting a pumpkin or bean seed.

● Let your children see you read for your own pleasure and interest and, if requested, answer questions about what you're reading. You may even be invited to read some of it out loud.

● Write something that can involve your children; a note on the fridge to buy more juice, a label or caption 'Jamie's Room. Keep out or the tiger will get you. Rrrrrr.'

- Write something that you need to write; a letter, shopping list, message etc. and be prepared to answer questions or give explanations.

- Play games with clues; 'I spy something that begins with "w". There are two of them in this room and you look through them.' 'I'm thinking of someone who is frightened of spiders. She ate curds and whey.' 'I'm round and sugary with currants in, you can eat me for your tea.'

Encourage your children to make up clues too.

- Provide materials (paper, pencils, textas, glue, scissors, magazines etc.) so that your children can explore these media and use their increasing manipulative and language skills to make their own picture stories.

Remember though this must be enjoyable. It is only 'natural' if your children want to do it. It should be fun for you and your children and it should only last as long as your children's interest does.

CHAPTER 7

That Sign says
'HAMBURGERS HERE'

—————— Lolly-wrap Literacy ——————

Some children fall passionately in love with the concept of language and collect words and phrases like other kids collect stamps. Some kids learn language on a 'need to know' basis. They are the survival readers.

Some parents think these children can't read. But they can read. They read lolly-wraps. And if you are in doubt wave a Mars Bar in front of their nose and their little eyes light up and they'll tell you if you bought the pack with 25% extra.

Lolly-wrap literacy starts in small ways with chockie frogs and icecream. But once out of the pusher their reading and eating taste varies. They move on to Twisties, Smarties, Minties and potato chips — plain and crinkle cut. From there they develop a taste for serious contemporary confection including KitKats, Cherry Ripes, Crunchies, Mars Bars and

Cool Mints. The next step is fast food literature. They can read menus. They know about Snak packs and Hawaiian packs, special offers and tubs. They become multi-cultural readers. They can read meat pies, french fries, dim sim, spring roll, Pepsi, pizza, Coke and gelati.

These kids are not only literate in five aisles of the supermarket, they can tell you the vintage and make of muesli bars by the competition advertised on the pack. And they can tell you the nutritional breakdown of Coco Pops.

Such children don't need special literacy training. It doesn't take them long to work out how to add a few words to the proper nouns such as 'I want Coco Pops.' And pretty soon they are able to write a four page dissertation on the significance of microwave technology.

They may not have read much Shakespeare, but you can guarantee they will have read every frozen pizza pack in the freezer. Shakespeare had a lot to say of value, but compared with the complete works of Poppa's Pizza, and I hate to say it, he's just not in the race.

You read that writing don't you?　　　　　Claire 3

Have you ever looked at your children in amazement as they show some spark of genius. They do or say something that you didn't know they could do and you say, 'How on earth do they know that?' 'Wherever did they get that from?'

The chances are that they've learned it quite naturally and spontaneously, and incidently when something sparks an interest or arouses curiosity. The activities have not been pre-planned or formal. They can't be. And yet, they are very powerful.

Kaye opened the air-mail envelope she had just received from her mother. Gary (aged 4) asked 'Is it from Gran?' Kaye said yes, and before she could start reading it Gary 'read' it for her.

'It says "Dear Kaye, Doug and Gary, the weather has been awful, love Mum, hugs and kisses!"'
Kaye was surprised at how much he knew about what might

have been in the letter. He had in fact almost read it. She shouldn't have been surprised though, because everytime a letter or card arrives she reads it to Gary. She just never realised before how much Gary was learning from the experiences.

Sharing a letter is just one example of a spontaneous activity. Let's look closer at it and see what Gary had gained from it. He had learned that:

o letters bring messages;
o letters are arranged in a special way that can be predicted;
o O's can mean hugs and X's can mean kisses;
o reading makes it possible to receive special messages;
o writing makes it possible to send special messages.

He may also have learnt to recognise some words and letters. The most important thing is that he had been learning spontaneously and naturally. He was relaxed and interested. He was not being taught, so felt no stress or pressure to perform. He was free to attend to those aspects that interested him, in this case form and content.

So what's so special about spontaneous activities? Most important is that they are not pre-planned teaching activities or lessons. They are not a substitute for school nor are they in conflict with what goes on in school later. They are informal situations that may arise at anytime from almost any situation. They are special to the children. From the children's involvement in these activities comes curiosity, motivation, a need to know and a need to do. The learning that arises therefore is meaningful and relevant to the children. It starts with the children, with their interest. The children decide how far they want to go with the activity. The children repeat, extend, redirect or cease the activity to suit their needs.

'I don't want to do that anymore.'   Jan

You need to be careful not to force learning out of a situation; just attend to your children's needs. Don't persist with an activity once interest has waned. Don't teach. Let learning happen.

Kate and Jamie were playing shop. They were both shopkeepers so Mum was called on to be the shopper. Mum got a bag and her purse and went shopping. But Kate was not satisfied. This had to be realistic. Mum had to have a shopping list. Mum got her pencil and paper and began to write.

'What's that say?' asked Jamie.

'Butter' said mum. 'What else do I need?'

Together a list of five items was made and shopping could begin. The list had to be given to the shopkeepers now who 'read' most of it. Help was needed on the middle item. Mum didn't say the whole word, just sounded the first letter and Kate and Jamie supplied the rest.

The spontaneous learning did not stop there. Several days later Kate and Jamie played shop again and tried to write their own lists. These were an assortment of pictures, zig zags and one or two real letters. But they were strikingly list-like. They hadn't written all across the page, just down one side. Mum who'd listened as the items were being represented, wrote her own shopping list including all those items. She again visited the shop and presented her list. Jamie seeing that orange juice began with O put an O in front of the scribble that represented orange juice on his list. He looked very satisfied with the outcome.

These shopping games demonstrate that children are very creative. They use what they've experienced to create their own games and in this case shopping lists. They learn naturally. They want to learn. Here the motivation was to be a shopper just like mum. They used the knowledge they'd gained in their own way. They decided what they needed and the timing was vital. They learnt what they wanted when it was important and valuable to them. So remember spontaneous activities should:

o not become teaching experiences;
o let kids be in the driving seat, deciding what they want to know or do;
o allow children to be creative;
o allow children to learn naturally when it's important to them

It says 'open other side'. You always start the wrong end.   Spiro

Spontaneous activities arise from many everyday situations. For example, when you:

o read instructions;
o choose a recipe;
o choose a television programme/cassette/record;
o go shopping;
o buy petrol;
o read the paper;
o go to the bank or post office;
o look up a phone number.

Children will be around you asking,
   'What are you doing?'
   'Why?'
   'What's it say?'
   'Where does it say Sesame Street?'
   'What's this letter?'
   'Why is this in big letters?'
From these activities the children will be learning some very important understandings about print, understandings that are essential if we want children to come to school prepared for learning to read. They will be learning that the squiggles on the page are words and letters, which, for example, can be used to convey all sorts of information. They will also be learning that there are conventions in print, like large letters for headings, capital letters at the beginning of sentences. They may also begin to:
o mimic the style;
o retell the message;
o identify some words or letters;
o ask questions that show they are really trying to understand the message.

These are all aspects that are essential to a smooth path towards reading and wanting to read.

Tom was cooking, Jemma wanted to help. Tom was being unusually patient for an elder brother. 'Okay' he pointed to the word flour. 'We need flour. Do you think you can find the container that says flour?' Jemma looked at the word flour in the recipe and then found the container that said flour. This was repeated for sugar too. She lost interest in cooking when Tom began measuring and mixing, preferring to re-read flour and sugar over and over. She traced her finger over the words. Then she tried to find them in the list of ingredients again. She spotted the word flour further down the page too and decided to scan the page to see if it was written elsewhere. She completed her task in time to demand a taste before the cake was put into the oven. Later that day she showed her Mum and Dad that she could read. She read flour and sugar.

It would have been easy to have used this moment to try to 'teach' some of the other words too. But that could have taken away the need to master just two words and may have resulted in no words being learned. Even more seriously it may have tarnished the natural learning. The child perceiving that mastery of the words was important to you could experience pressure and stress, the desire to please taking its toll on spontaneous learning.

By their very nature spontaneous activities just happen.

o Sorting old photos can give rise to wanting a scrap book with labels and captions;
o cutting up old magazines will do the same;
o planting a row of seeds may call for reading the packet, making a label for the row;
o a journey gives rise to sign reading, street names, spotting a take away food place;
o preparing clothes and accessories for preschool will mean name and address tags.

If children's questions and attempts at reading are responded to they will quite naturally generate many more. So many in fact you may want to turn the record off.
In summary:

o Resist the temptation to teach or direct rather, let children learn naturally.
o Let the children take the driving seat, deciding the what, when and how themselves.
o Spontaneous activity provides meaningful contexts for reading and writing.
o Spontaneous activity can arise from all sorts of common day to day activities.

Activities

Well obviously if these activities are to be spontaneous they can't be listed here! So instead here's an awareness list to help you spot those potential spontaneous activities.

● Listen, really listen to your children.

● Let them know that you like them asking questions by taking time (when it's practicable) to really answer the questions asked.

● Observe your children's interests, e.g. cars, play shop, dressing up and capitalise on these by extending their interests. Spot car makes, number plates, garages and related signs when you go out. Introduce these into games at home. You could make speed signs, stop signs etc. Provide materials for the 'shop', empty packets, washed empty tins, juice containers, till dockets, shopping lists and a customer for the shop. Extend dressing up by introducing lots of characters in books and stories and looking at and talking about characters on television and videos.

● Provide many joint experiences, gardening, cooking, shopping, playing games, going to the garage, car wash, reading a map, visiting the park that will generate chat, questions and use of environmental print.

CHAPTER 8

Imagination Unlimited

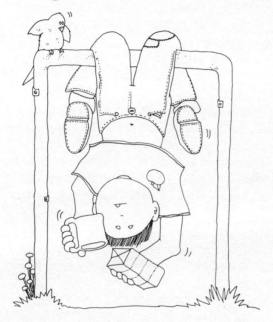

—— Mary Had a Little…Giggle…Giggle… ——

Not restrained by convention nor trapped within the boundaries of formal education, children have the most brilliantly vivid and absurdly wild imaginations imaginable.

We grown-ups like to think our imaginations have grown with us, but I tend to think they have been channelled in certain directions. And I feel this absolutely when I'm invited briefly to share the turbulent and vivid world of a child's imagination.

'Open my face,' requested my two-year-old. 'I want to see my bones.'

'I love all of you,' I said to my son when he was three. 'You have to love all of me,' he said with an air of impatience.

'You couldn't just cuddle a head.'

'Can gravity go up?' asked son at five.

Of course, being unrestrained by convention, children's minds often stray into areas parents prefer to keep 'off limits'. 'Mary had a little...(expletive deleted)', sang one member of the family. I might add that this version of the song would have had serious-minded kindergarten teachers fainting in the street.

'Where did you learn that?' I asked.

'I made it up all by myself,' came the honest and totally innocent reply.

We parents held our breath. And the child's imagination soon raced on to new and more exhilarating events.

This was most fortunate as our parental imaginations had already shot ahead along a fairly predictable path to mayhem, and were in fear that our child was going to become famous for writing the X-rated version of *Mother Goose*.

The clock struck two. The mouse said poo (giggle giggle)
Hickory Dickory Dock   Julia 4

Imagination develops and is nurtured by the experiences that children have. It reflects and interprets the various sensory experiences that children have. It is impossible to imagine and recall the smell of fish and chips if you've never actually smelt them. It is hard to imagine and make up rhythms and songs if you've never heard any. And how could you imagine and re-live the taste of a gobstopper if you'd never had one. Without words, pictures and stories there would be no beautiful princesses, ghosts or goblins to imagine.

Fired by our experiences we can project what we know, what we have met, into other situations. We can combine sensations, stories and pictures to create yet more situations and stories and pictures.

This is precisely what children do in their play and in their drawings when they create multi-storey car parks, shops, hospitals, mums and dads, cops and robbers, goodies and baddies, Batman, space travel that reflect their own experiences. People they've met, places they've been, stories they've heard, television shows they've seen all provide fuel for this developing imagination.

Imagination is a vital part of the child's development. Imagination makes it possible for children to have excitement, adventure, to pretend what it would be like to be some one else or somewhere else. Through imagination children can lose themselves for a while and even confront their fears in the safety of a game.

Imagination can be extended by the use of descriptive language and by metaphor. As you talk and play with your children things you say and point out will help them extend their imaginations.

'The clouds look like white fluffy sheep.'

'When you talk like that you sound like Max when he got mad.'

In response to these inputs children will use metaphor too. They'll look at things and see other things in them.

Imagination has a two way thrust in the development of literacy. Without imagination most of the stories in books will be hard to engage with. Without imagination you can't put yourself in the role of the characters. You can't associate with, empathise with them, love or hate them. You can't predict or anticipate what they might feel, think or do next. Without imagination you can't visualise or really visit the places in the story. You can't smell and hear the jungle. You can't anticipate the danger, excitement or humour. So a limited imagination means a limited enjoyment of the wonderful world of books. A limited enjoyment of books results in a limited interest in books and so a limited drive to want to read.

Not only do we need imagination to really enjoy books. We also need books to fire our imagination. Stories in books provide new places, new characters, new adventures, for children to savour and incorporate into their repertoire of games. As children play and try out the characters and situations they are making sense of their world. They are putting themselves in other people's shoes, feeling what they feel, knowing what they know. They are also creating new stories and characters. They are rehearsing and preparing for later writing and reading tasks. Children who can imagine, visualise and predict what's in a book on the basis of their story knowledge. They can also use this knowledge to predict what to include in their own stories.

You be the witch. I'll be Snow White.

The stories children make up and act out are based on real events or just as frequently stories that have been read to them. The richness and complexity of these stories will reflect the experiences and books that the children have shared. Stories that have been read or told to the children provide them with expectations about what a story is, how it's organised (beginning, middle, end), how stories are read expressively, how language (words, rhythms, rhymes), are used to give life to a story, how the picture matches the text. In turn this information and experience is used as the children create, tell or illustrate their own stories and later it is used to help children predict and anticipate as they begin to read.

Run, Run as fast as you can. You can't catch me I'm a giant man
Ben 3

Repetitive stories, rhyming stories, nursery rhymes and poems provide the stimulus and models for children to create their own rhymes and to invent play situations. Kids are creative language users. They enjoy hearing and creating jingles and nonsense

— *giggle glog, giggle glog,*
— *piggle pog, piggle pog.*   Amanda 4

When children play with language to create new words or nonsense rhymes they are trying their knowledge of rhythm, rhyme, sounds and language use. Knowledge which is invaluable in the reading process. So:

o foster and value these early creative language games;

o encourage these early explorations of literary style;
o feed the children more stories, rhymes, jingles and tongue twisters;
o have fun together inventing some more;
o enjoy your child's creativity.

Here's the caterpillar on the leaf and he's eating olives.　　Ben 4

Imagination and story knowledge are involved when children draw their own pictures. The illustrations in the book may stimulate the activity but it is the child's imagination and interpretation that shines through into their illustrations. Drawing and describing pictures is an important step toward the writing of stories.

In summary then, imagination is not innate. It needs fostering, nurturing and fuelling. Encourage your children to be imaginative. Many children create themselves imaginary playmates, make up extremely tall stories, draw often unrecognisable but very imaginative story pictures. Value this activity. Let your children see that it's okay behaviour. It is not mere day dreaming, it's not telling lies and it's not just scribble. It is a vital step towards wanting to read and write and therefore to becoming a reader and writer.

Activities

• Tell some tall or at least imaginative stories.

• Read some stories to your children.

• Dress up and act out the stories.

CHAPTER 9

'Mum, you're the Dragon. O.K.?'

What's Wrong with Quiet Creative Play?

There are two ways children play. First of all, there is the what-are-those-two-up-to-now quiet play, which involves diabolical mischief and secrecy. This is not creative play. It is closer to creative devastation. The children are either squishing their way through their mother's make-up kit, feeding the goldfish Weet Bix or cleaning the toilet bowl with boot polish.

And while parents would like to respond to this sort of play by launching themselves into an hysterical rendition of an adult tantrum, they can't as the big eyes look up at them and the little devastator says 'I help!'

Then there is creative play. It can be quiet. I know this as I snuck up on my children one time, drawn by the heavy silence coming from their end of the house. But they were being creative. They were playing 'Dead Bodies'.

'You be the dead body.'

'OK.'

SILENCE

By and large I must say my children prefer creative havoc. Not only do they opt for noisy games — swash-buckling pirate games, super heroes saving the planet games (super heroes are super noisy), interstellar war games, doctors and hysterical patient games and unsynchronised acrobatic troupe games and so on — they also try to involve me in the plot.

Against my will I become a mountain, or a satellite or a friendly alien or a horse. I'm also nominated referee and asked to make a decision on who actually predeceased whom at the OK Cosmic Corral.

Unfortunately my contribution goes largely unappreciated because even as a mountain I demonstrate a certain lack of concentration by constantly moving. Actually my only success at directing quiet creative play was when I sent participants off on an arduous mission a long, long way away from Mother Earth. I hate to admit this, but it was cosmic bliss.

Children's play is actually a very serious business. As kids play they might be:

o trying out new roles;
o fantasising;
o having a real adventure;
o acting out stories or making up stories.

They might also be trying out new skills like:

o balancing;
o skipping;
o counting;
o shopping;
o cutting and pasting;
o reading and writing.

As children play they are in many ways feeling their way into the grown up world. They play at 'schools'. Bits of paper, pencils, chalk, and teddies are all brought together as part of the game and an approximation of school takes place. If there is an older sibling around then some real reading and writing may take place. As the game unfolds, stories will be told or 'read', roles will be rehearsed and modified. If you are invited to join in, some spontaneous reading and writing will occur.

Games of this type provide opportunities for the children to draw on their own knowledge of, for example, school. They know that you read and write at school and so 'reading' and 'writing' are part of the game. They may associate learning letters with going to school, and so will fetch their magnetic letters or alphabet books for their lesson. You may be required to write the letters for them. Incidental and spontaneous learning is part of this type of game. The children are setting their own tasks and learning as they play.

Michael had just come out of hospital and was going to grow up to be a doctor. He had his Mum's white shirt, his dad's clipboard, two cotton reels on a bit of string, and his soft toys. Day after day he played doctors. Each toy had his name tag on, just as Michael had in hospital. Each toy had a record sheet at the foot of its bed, just as Michael had had. Michael had the spice jars as pill bottles. Each day a fresh piece of paper for each patient had to have the day written on it and the date. Michael tried copying the day and date onto his clipboard along with his patients names. His Mum and Dad had to record the temperatures and what the patients had eaten on each sheet. Ailments had to be invented and recorded. Michael was compulsive about this game and wouldn't look at his other toys at all. Cheryl said they played it with Michael in case his trip into hospital had been very disturbing for him. But after a few days they noticed that Michael was really reading the record sheets and name tags and was able to write the names of the toys unaided.

Michael had been really fascinated by his hospital stay. He'd questioned the nurses and doctors and his parents the whole time. His interest in doctors continued for many weeks after he went home. As well as playing at being a doctor he quite naturally and easily began to read and write as part of his make believe game. His parents didn't 'teach' him nor did they direct or takeover his games. They just joined in when invited and provided any information or writing that he required. The whole process was natural and the learning that took place 'on the job' was used as part of the game. The same few words were seen and used several times a day for many days. The words were actually needed and used as part of the game. The words were particularly special to Michael at that time. Michael was relaxed, interested and motivated to learn. And learn he did, all on his own.

As adults we need to learn how to help children play. That doesn't mean joining in and taking over. That means knowing:

o when to join in;
o how to join in;
o what contribution to make;
o how to stimulate further play.

If you joined in without being invited when your children are playing with their cars and started to organise the game 'better' — 'Right, I'll have these cars, you have these and we'll send them to each other' — this might be fun for a little while or it might not be accepted at all. In either instance the children have been encroached on and the game has not been extended in any way.

It is better to:

o wait to be invited;
o ask questions or retell shared experiences ('Where does this road go to?' 'I remember when we took you to the park and there were fire-engines everywhere.');
o next time you are out point out details or events that would add to the game (road signs, the route on a map, putting petrol in);
o read some books with cars as a theme (e.g. *Gumdrop, Going Shopping*);

The pushing of cars might then be extended to making a road

map and signs to push the cars on, a trip to the homemade garage for petrol or extensions where print (reading and writing) are part of the game.

I'm drawing some writing   Sam 4

Many of the games that children play could at some stage involve the need for paper and pens. Sam, when he wanted a shop but had nothing to sell was quite happy to draw. He drew butter, eggs, money and labels. His labels were scribble writing, but he knew what they meant and they worked well in his game. If you are playing trains you might need tickets and money. If you are playing banks you need forms. A constant supply of paper and pens will make it possible for children to add these extras to their games. You will probably be called on to write the money, tickets and signs, or to be the person using the ones made by the children. These are valuable situations where reading and writing can be demonstrated and seen as purposeful.

You be the Princess, and I'll be the bad bad witch.

Not all games are based in the real world. The stories you read to your children, tales you tell them, and things they see on television can generate fantasy games.

Richard and Edward watched the seeds from the pumpkin being discarded and asked if they could have some to plant. They took them outside deciding who would be the old woman. The old woman it transpired would water them and put chook poo on them. After the planting and the words 'grow plant grow', always uttered after planting in this household, they sat and watched. They went off and came back. Still no signs of growth.

'Oh well' said Edward 'we'll have to magic it.'

'Let's pretend,' said Richard.

Together they heaved and heaved chanting, 'and they pulled and they pulled and they pulled' as they did so. They called for their dog and two cats to help. The dog and cats never came. Richard and Edward finally pulled out the enormous pumpkin and 'cooked' it in the muddy patch they were calling their kitchen today.

As the children play these sorts of games they are using their story knowledge, in this instance *The Enormous Turnip*, and their understanding of the characters. They are also using the language of stories in a literary way to create their play. As they play they retell the story exactly, or they change parts to suit their own ends. This is early reading behaviour. The children are beginning to talk like a book. They know stories have a beginning, a problem and a resolution or ending, so these features become a feature of their games. They are in fact creating and rehearsing their own stories. Modifying bits if they don't like them. This type of play is the first stage of children having their own stories to write. It's also a key part of later literary appreciation. Only by trying out the roles and the situations can you begin to think about questions like,

'Why did X do that?'

'What would you have done?'

These questions are part of understanding and appreciating literature. As they play the children are also using descriptive language from books. They know a 'dragon' is a pale insignificant thing by comparison with 'a fearsome toothsome dragon'. Often as they play, they play with language too. And as they play they are bringing their books to life. They can have the fun, the adventures, the sorrow, the jokes in the safety of the game. And as they play they'll be hungry for more books, more characters, more adventures. So stoke their fires with lots and lots of story books. Make them want to read them for themselves too.

In summary, take a fresh look at kids play and remember:

o play is serious work;
o reading and writing can be a natural part of a game;
o join in the play when invited but do not direct or takeover;
o provide stimulus (outings, books, discussion) to extend subsequent play sessions;
o provide paper and pens as part of the play kit;

o stories are a great source of kids fantasy play ideas;
o fantasy play is part of literacy development where children rehearse and create their own stories;
o fantasy play provides scope for playing with literary language too;
o and try not to worry about the 'mess' for a while. It's impossible to have a good game without adequate space. Sometimes it's good to be able to leave a game up overnight.

Activities

● Think of some play situations that you could involve your children in e.g. hospitals, space travel, the office, school, jungle adventure. Sometimes children need an idea to start them off.

● Read lots of stories with different settings and different problems to your children so that these can become integrated into their games.

● Make up some playkits using scrap materials, e.g. packets and cans for a shop, large cardboard boxes for the construction of garages, puppet theatres, houses, farms, shops, cars, boats or planes;

● Decorate large brown paper bags to make, monster masks, puppets, dressing-up clothes;

● Use old sheets to make a tent, cubby house, ghost's outfit, princess or bride, train, picnic mat, or even the sail on a pirate boat;

● Watch Play School together and try out their play ideas;

● Demonstrate or tell stories about games you played as a child;

● Invite some friends to play with your children perhaps with the specific aim of playing pirates, schools, Star Wars or monsters so that they can be invited to come dressed up as the part.

CHAPTER 10

Once Upon an Educationally Sound Period When Times Were Dull

——— Not Another Noodle Eating Poodle ———

If Dr Seuss were to make a public appearance in Australia, he would be besieged by parents with bricks in box and rocks in sox wanting to beat him about the middle with a paddle in a puddle. And I would lead the bitter battle hurling a bottle at the noodle eating poodle.

As you can gather I am not fond of noodle eating poodles. Or Dr Seuss books. It wasn't always so. I loved Dr Seuss. But *The Fox in Sox* finished me off. It wasn't the first reading...or even the eighth reading, but about the 23rd reading that I cried 'I cannot stand one more tweetle beetle

battle in a bottle. I hate tweetle beetles. I hate bottle bat-
tles. And that's it.' So we converted to *The Cat in the Hat*.

It amazed me that children can become so addicted to
one book. A friend's son was a *Cat in the Hat* addict. It
went on for months. Then finally he went to school. He came
skipping out the gate saying,

'It's really great Mum. We can take books out of the library.'

His mother smiled. Then she opened his library bag to
discover a battered school edition of *The Cat in the Hat*.

There is a lesson here for all parents. Children can have
quite different tastes in books to their parents. Or so I have
come to realise. I love all of those sweet little pixies-and-
bunnies-romping-in-fairyland books. But my first born
prefers adventure stories. Knights. Robots. Blood-sucking
vampires. Dark caverns. Evil pits. He might not get night-
mares, but I thought I would. So we have compromised. One
noble-knight-questing-against-the-foul-and-sinister-
forces-of-evil book for him. One gay-little-pixie-tripping-
through-the-enchanted-wood book for Mum.

And in that way, if I have a nightmare, it involves Tinkerbell defending the universe against the combined forces of
evil. And I know Tinkerbell will win.

I want you to read me TWENTY stories.   Edward

Throughout this book we have emphasised the importance of
reading regularly to our children right from birth. The benefits
children gain from regular reading include:

o a rich and varied vocabulary
o an understanding of what reading is and how books work
o an increased imagination
o a range of experiences that they could never have actually had
  themselves
o a broad general knowledge

o hours and hours of pleasure and the promise of many more pleasurable hours to come
o a positive attitude to reading and motivation to want to read themselves

---

Baby: 'Dog'
Mum: 'Yes, a spotty dog.'

There are many books that are especially designed with babies in mind and others that will have qualities that make them suitable for the very first years. Cloth books, bath books (plastic, foam filled ones) and board books stand up to the rigours of tiny hands, gums and teeth. They also of course offer pictures of objects or things of special appeal to babies and toddlers as well as simple stories. Books like *Pets*, Valerie Greely (familiar pets); *Little Numbers*, Rodney Peppe (all about toys); *Good Morning*, Dick Bruna (daily events) are closely linked to the world and natural curiosity of the young child.

The first words babies learn are the names of things in their surroundings. Books like these provide the stimulus for increasing this range of words and lead into captions and sentences.

Many of the books in the Ladybird series are designed for use with very young children. These can withstand a fair amount of handling too. Look-out for their 'Talk about books', their picture books and their rhyme books. There is sure to be a book that suits your pocket and need. Some titles to look for are

Baby's First Book
Talk about Animals
Talk about Home
Talk about Shopping
Nursery Rhyme Books 1, 2 and 3
Bedtime Rhymes

Children want to touch, feel and suck everything. Books like these can be shared with your children and they can also have the pleasure of handling the books too. It is very important to include books that can be handled in your infant's library.

The 'Spot' books have great appeal to tiny fingers and eyes and are fairly durable. Each book tells a simple story asking questions like 'Who's behind the door?' which invite children to lift the flap and see. It's rather like playing 'Peek a Boo'. Titles in this series by Eric Hill include *Spot's First Walk, Where's Spot?, Spot's Birthday Party, Spot's First Christmas.*

There are less durable books too that young children will love. Noisy books are popular, books like, *Bertie and the Bear*, Pamela Allen; *I Can Roar*, Frank Asch; *See Mouse Run*, Sally Grindly and Priscilla Lamont; *Goodnight Owl*, Pat Hutchins; *Peepo*, Janet and Allen Ahlberg.

A general guide is, if you enjoy the book, your enjoyment and enthusiasm will be caught. Make story time a cosy, cuddly, funtime for your baby or toddler.

As children grow older (2–5 years) there is a vast range of books available. Children need to experience this variety. Books with wonderful illustrations, bright ones, detailed ones, realistic ones, wishy washy ones, complicated ones, cartoon ones, and pop up ones. They need to hear the whole range of rich language and varied language patterns. They need to experience books that offer excitement, adventure, humour and emotions. They offer a safe place where children can explore their fears, try out other peoples' roles and broaden their view of the world. They need to learn to love books.

I don't want them to live happily ever after.

What follows is a guide to the variety of books available and the special features of each type of book. We begin with story books, books that you might choose with no motive other than to introduce terrific stories and illustrations to your children. Some of these are all time classics like the Beatrix Potter Books

The Little Engine that Could   retold by Watty Piper
Little Tim and the Brave Sea Captain   Edward Ardizzone
Harry the Dirty Dog   Gene Zion
Harry By the Sea   Gene Zion
Mike Mulligan and His Steam Shovel   Virginia Lee Burton
The Story About Ping   Marjorie Flack
The Story of Babar, The Little Elephant   Jean de Brunhoff.

You may even still have your own copies to read to your children. How wonderful. Many recent books have become classics in their own time. Books like

Mog the Forgetful Cat Judith Kerr
Frog and Toad All Year Round Arnold Lobel
The Bad Tempered Ladybird Eric Carle
Possum Magic Mem Fox
The Balloon Tree Phoebe Gilman
Alexander's Terrible, Horrible, No Good,
Very Bad Day Judith Viorst
The Tiger Who Came to Tea Judith Kerr.

Include some folk stories and fairy tales too. Books like

A Piece of Straw Junko Marimoto
The Puffin Children's Treasury

Books of the type listed here are to be savoured, to be read over and over again. A simple rule when choosing story books is to sample them before you buy them. Stand in the shop and read some or all of the book. Does it have a strong story line? Is the language rich and evocative? Are the characters believable? Do you like the illustrations? Do the illustrations match or add to the text? Did you enjoy the sampling? Do you think your children will like it? If you answer yes to these questions the chances are you're on to a winner. Take it home and invite it to become one of your friends. Initially choose the shorter books but increase your children's listening span by introducing longer stories over time. In addition to loving books children need to be able to join in with some of them. There are books around that as well as being terrific picture story books also have repetitive lines that are an open invitation to children to join in. Books like

Goodnight Owl! Pat Hutchins
where most pages end with 'and owl tried to sleep'
Mister Magnolia Quentin Blake
which repeats 'But Mr Magnolia has only one boot.'

Joining in is important because it ensures that the children use the language of the book. They listen carefully for the cue and enjoy their moment. Soon they begin to notice where on the page their line comes, and if you point as you go will begin to match the written words with the spoken ones. The repetition of the words, and of course the repeated readings provides the exposure to the words that are needed for your children to recognise those words. In effect this is drill and practice but in an enjoyable setting.

In the Middle of the Night by Amanda Graham has a text that is repetitive. The only new words required are either clearly signalled by the pictures, or depend on the ability to count. A book like this very quickly makes a child feel like a reader. Children can use the repetition, the counting and the strong picture cues to help them retell the story. The repetitive lines will be parrotted and the children will begin to recognise some of the words. Children remember the meaningful, rhythmic parts of stories very easily. Later they begin to remember the less memorable lines. As they begin to recall more of a text word for word so they move closer to being able to 'read' it. There will come a day when the book can be 'read' word perfectly from cover to cover. Next will come the day when each spoken word is matched to each printed word. 'Reading' is on the way. Strong picture cues make this recall easier, providing any necessary prompts. Later picture cues will help your children work out unknown words in stories they are reading themselves. This is an important early reading strategy that can begin right now. So draw attention occasionally to the way the picture cues the story. The sequence of the counting numbers in this story also acts as a cue for the story. Encourage your children to use their counting knowledge to predict the next page of the book.

Some books have a small vocabulary and a repetitive quality that make them easy to join in with and to recognise some of the words. *Nicky's Noisy Night* by Harriet Ziefert is a lift-a-flap book of this type. As each flap is lifted there are words to describe each noise, the branch goes 'tap, tap', the mouse goes 'squeak', the dustbin goes 'crash bang'. This is an added bonus because children love 'noisy' books. They enjoy predicting what the noise might be and then joining in, again a good way to promote reading behaviour.

Cumulative books combine the repetitive lines with a story that adds to the lines page by page. You may remember examples of this type from your own childhood, books like *The Gingerbread Man and The Enormous Turnip*. You may even recall the lines, so powerful are these types of stories.

Run, run as fast as you can.
You can't catch me I'm the Gingerbread Man.

The Fat Cat by Jack Dent is an example of this type where a greedy cat, page by page, adds to the list of things he's already eaten...until you guessed it...someone comes to the rescue; a bit gruesome perhaps but the sort of thing children love. *Hattie and the Fox* by Mem Fox, is a book where not only does the text cumulate and repeat but also where the goose, pig, horse, sheep and cow all have repeating lines. A family can have great fun with this one.

Can I have a WELCOME on my door?

Some books have few words with very strong picture clues. The book can almost be read by looking at the pictures. This again is important in helping the children feel they are reading, can read. Children who perceive themselves as readers soon will read.

Monster Can't Sleep by Virginia Meuller is an example of this type of book and also includes a repeating line
'But Monster wasn't sleepy.'
And don't worry, Monster is a cutie.

I'm Going on a Dragon Hunt by Charlotte Firmin and *Go Ducks Go* by Maurice Burns also perfect this technique. Books with strong rhyme and rhythm also encourage joining in. Books like *Bertie and the Bear* by Pamela Allen, *Mr McGee* by Pamela Allen and *Hairy Maclary* by Lynley Dodd invite children to join in and to predict what the next word might be. Prediction is an important part of reading. When children begin reading, the process is much more fluent if they are predicting what's coming next. Children who are used to anticipating what's coming next, used to joining in with the rhythm and flow of a book, will expect to read like that too. The hard work of looking at, recognising or sounding out each word is unnecessary at the early stages of reading.

Not all books have words. Many just have beautiful illustrations that tell the story. Books like these encourage children to talk about the pictures and make up the story themselves. This is an essential part of early literacy development. The children look closely at the clues in the pictures picking out important details. They experiment with language to get the best effect. Children who can use pictures in this way will also be able to use pictures to help them retell the story or work out some of the unfamiliar words on the page. *The Snowman* by Raymond Briggs and *The Gift* by John Prater are two stories that have no words at all. *Rosie's Walk* by Pat Hutchins and *Doing the Washing* by Sarah Garland are books that have very few words. Much of the information needed to really appreciate these stories comes from the pictures. I call these 'Tell it Yourself' stories. Stories like these encourage creativity and allow the children's unique qualities to shine. And no! They are not just for the very young. I love them too. Young children often need a lot of prompts and assistance to tell these stories. Prompts like, 'Look what's happened', and 'What do you think will happen next?'

Some children are not prepared to tell the stories for these picture books in which case you can go to town on the story telling. Eventually your children will want to join in or tell the story themselves. To tell a story from pictures children use all their knowledge about stories. They sequence the events, use the language and language patterns of stories they've heard, incorporate bits of description and action. They may include humour and imagination. These are skills that children will then be able to bring to the stories that they tell, draw or write, an important feature of story writing.

I want a dinosaur in my garden and a plesiosaur in my bath too.

By reading and sharing books with your children you will be broadening their horizons, introducing them to places that they could never go and to people they could never meet. You will be stretching their imaginations.

In *A Pet for Mrs Arbuckle* by Gwenda Smyth and Ann James, Mrs Arbuckle goes on a journey around the world looking for a pet. She goes to Mexico looking for an armadillo, to Africa to see a giraffe, to Patagonia for a llama, to California to see a whale. Illustrations show each setting and animal, opening up a whole world of different places and landscapes. *Around the World with Ant and Bee* by Angela Banner is also a travel story which takes a journey around the world. Eric Carle's *Have You Seen My Cat?* is another travel story. In books like *The Knight and the Dragon*, Tomi De Paola; *I've Got a Secret*, Betty Evans; *The Shy Dragon*, Marie-Jose Sacre and Jindra Strnad we meet mythical dragons. Dinosaurs are met in books like *Long Neck and Thunderfoot*, Helen Peirs and *There's a Dinosaur in the Garden,* Michael Salmon. The jungle is visited in *The Proud and Fearless Lion*, Ann and Reg Cartwright. A train ride is taken in *Teddy Bears Take the Train*, Susanna Gretz and Alison Sage. And for those who haven't seen snow, *The Snowy Day* by Ezra Jack Keats says and shows it all.

Rrr Moo...I'm a liocow.

By reading books like these to your children you are broadening their horizons and their imaginations. To read any book themselves children need to have some experience and background related to the topic of the book. They also need to imagine what the book may be about, what kind of words and literary style will be used. By reading a variety of books to your children you are ensuring that they will have those experiences and the imagination required when they become beginner readers. There are books which will really stimulate the imagination. Books like

The Mixed Up Chameleon   Eric Carle
In the Night Kitchen   Maurice Sendak
Would You Rather Be a Bullfrog?   Theo Le Seig
One Dragon's Dream   Peter Pavey
are not only extremely imaginative but also demand an imaginative response.

Not all books are fiction and it is essential that we introduce children to a full range of books. In this section we look at alphabet books. Many of these use rhyme and alliteration as devices to make them more interesting. These include, *A — Z and Back Again*, Carol Mills, *Dr Seuss's A B C*, *Richard Scarry's A B C*. There are also ABC books that simply show illustrations and names of objects beginning with a particular letter such as those by John Burningham, Brian Wildsmith and Elizabeth Cleaver.

Many children love finding out about things. It is hard to find factual books for this age range. If your children have a particular interest, dinosaurs for instance, you may well find that they will listen to a book written for children well beyond their own years. It is important that children realise that not all books are story books. Books like the following have a universal appeal: *Baby Animals* photographed by Kathie Atkinson, *Ant Cities* by Arthur Dorros, *One Hungry Spider* by Jeannie Baker and *The Children's Picture Prehistory Dinosaurs* by Anne McCard.

They extend the children's interest and background knowledge. They increase their vocabulary by introducing specific terms like, extinct, arachnid, cat family, spin, web-terms that provide the background language and ideas needed to read other factual books. Children love playing with and using these words too. They soon become part of their spoken repertoire.

In summary, read often to your children. Make available a wide assortment of books. Select books that you enjoy too. Check that the books you buy or borrow are of suitable quality to make your children want to hear them time and time again.

Activities

So start right now,

- spread out the children's books you have and see how representative the range is. Do they include some fact, some fiction, some classics and so on. List the categories you'd like to add to so that when you visit book shops, garage sales, or the library you can decide what type of books to look for next;

- set time aside each day for reading, not just bedtime. Children are often alert early in the morning and could attend to a story. A sibling quarrel can be forgotten after reading a story. A tantrum can be diverted, a game can be stimulated by sharing stories;

- react to the stories, let your children see that they make you laugh, shock you, surprise you or make you sad;

- make some books of your own. They don't all have to be bought. You could make your own word books using magazines or catalogues. Funny people books and stories can be made by cutting and pasting magazine pictures. Old photos can make biographies or funny moment stories. Food wrappers can make meals for hungry giant books. Just use your imagination. The list is endless;

- tape some stories so that when you are busy your children can listen and follow their favourite stories on their own.

Together, enter the Aladdin's Cave of wonderful places, people, creatures and adventures that books hold in store for you.

CHAPTER 11

How Do I Use Books

'Let's Cut off the Queen's Head'

There is a fabulous game we have played with books. We only played it once, but it was fun at the time. (I don't want you to think I'm one of those overbearingly perfect parents who does absolutely everything with their children. I don't. I could be a perfect parent, mind you, if I didn't have to cook, clean, wash, earn an income and so forth. Unfortunately, I've had to postpone being a perfect parent until I can talk the family into giving up eating and getting dirty and that sort of thing.)

In the meantime, here is the game. First of all we cut off the Queen's head from a magazine. Cut off someone else's head if you are a royalist. Then turn through the pages of books plopping the head on other bodies. It's fun. Then do it with animals. We made a montage once and named the animals — snakearoo, kookakoala and so on. This, say the experts, is good for their imagination. Of course it sets their knowledge of zoology back ten years. But it is good for their imagination.

Read it in your funny voice.

There are no hard and fast rules about how to use books. There are however reasons for using books that need to be considered, reasons that will affect the way you read different books at different times. The main reason of course is to invite your children to enjoy and choose to listen to the magic that books contain. This is the key to developing not just readers, but life-long readers. It is also the key to developing

o imagination
o curiosity
o understanding (of the world)
o a wide vocabulary and language use
o a broad range of background experiences
o a desire to join in with the reading
o a strong motivation to want to read.

Whatever the book or purpose for reading it, have fun, relax, be spontaneous and let yourself go. See what happens. But do remember, these books are for sharing. Don't make your children join in. Don't have expectations about what they should do, or about how they should respond. Read to your children, involve them and make space for them to join in or comment if they want to.

Can we have Hansel and Gretel again?

There are guidelines that may help you ensure that your children get the maximum pleasure and benefit from a book. Story-books for instance enlist all the skills of the storyteller. Tone and pacing, facial expression and gestures can be used to bring stories to life. The first step with storybooks is to get your children involved, to draw them into the book, to set the mood and make your children feel curious about the story and characters. For example,

'This story is about two children who have a stepmother who doesn't love them. She wants to get rid of them. You listen and see what happens'.

'Is that what witches really sound like Mum? Are you a witch?'

Expressive and dramatic reading makes the characters real, creates vivid images and entices the children. The effect of this can be strengthened if your partner reads some of the story too. For example the witch in Hansel and Gretel. Ham it up. Let your face show the moods of the characters. Let it show how you are feeling (frightened, sad, happy). Let your children know that feelings are aroused when you read books. They need to know that it's okay to become totally involved with the characters and the plot. Encourage them to talk about their feelings too. Choose books that arouse all sorts of moods and feelings. Together you can laugh at the humour, gasp at the element of surprise, feel sad if things are not going well, rejoice in the safe or happy ending.

After you read the storybooks talk about them. Talk about the character, the plot, the ending, the parts you each like best. Compare stories you have shared. You could ask,

'What other stories do we know that have a happy ending?'
'What other animal stories have we read?'
'Do you think this story is like any other story we know?'
'How many animals are chasing Crunch, Mum?'

Talk about the illustrations and take time to look closely at them after reading the story. Perhaps use them to help in a retelling of the story. Remember, some stories will be quite wordy and may not invite joining in. They may also demand a lot of concentration from your children. You may need to serialise some of the longer ones.

A cautionary note: do not read too quickly. If a story is to be really understood and listened to by your children you need to read fairly slowly so that they can:

o listen to and enjoy the words;
o visualise people, places and scenes;
o anticipate what is coming next;
o savour what has just passed.

Comprehension is dependent on these aspects. If the words are garbled, the ideas or events coming too quickly, then much of the meaning and pleasure will be lost. The enthusiasm and gusto with which you bring your children's books to life will emphasise the language of the books, differentiate the characters, and set the scene. Above all it will help your children to listen to the stories, to play with the stories using them as part of their own imaginative play and story telling, and to want to participate more fully in the dramatisation of them.

Can I be the General who Toots?

Expressive and dramatic reading is a vital part of reading joining-in type books too.

Some books, though intended as story books, go beyond telling, they positively invite children to join in with the words, the rhymes, the rhythm and the repetition. The characters themselves may also invite them to join in, as in Sally Grindley's *Knock, Knock, Who's There?*. There are only really two characters in this book, the daughter and the father. The father, however pretends to be first a gorilla, then a witch, then a ghost, then a dragon, then a giant and finally is himself.

After hearing this story two or three times children begin to join in with the 'knock, knock', the 'Who's there?' and 'Well you can't come in!' If you point to the words as your children are saying them they will begin to see the relationship between the written word and the spoken word. They will notice that 'knock, knock' is two words and that both words look the same and they will begin to recognise these words by their shape, possibly by their first and last letters. Focus on the words and word recognition can become part of a game in this book. For example you could say, 'Dad must have sore knuckles after knocking on the door so much. Let's see how many knocks he made.' This provides a reason for looking at the words, highlighting that each of the clusters is one word and matching the spoken and written words. This is an important first step in the process of becoming a reader. Asking how many times the girl says 'Who's there?' or 'Well then you can't come in' provides further opportunities to develop word recognition. This type of word spotting and word recognition should be a joint, non-threatening spontaneous activity.

Be the Turramulli, Dad.

Knock, knock also offers great scope for children to experiment with descriptive language, and to change the story characters. Act out the story with your children, them in bed and you behind the door and then invite them to suggest characters from books, or TV that you can dramatise.

They might suggest characters like the wicked queen in Walt Disney's *Snow White*, the fairy godmother in *Sleeping Beauty* the fox from *Rosie's Walk* or Crunch from *Crunch the Crocodile*. Alternatively your children may want to dress up and or dramatise these characters themselves. Use your children's suggestions to create a new version of the book. In large writing record their descriptions and staple these into a book. Because this new version reflects your children's interests and experiences, and because it uses their own language, they will not only be motivated to read it repeatedly themselves but will also be able to 'read' it because it reflects exactly what they want to say.

Teddy Bear's Moving Day by Susanne Gretz is another type of joining-in book. Here it is the speech and thought bubbles that so fascinate children. After pointing to the bubbles and explaining their purpose to the children, they very quickly want to 'read' that part, especially if on first reading the 'I Do' 'I Do Not's' were read in loud cross voices. When the children join in encourage them to really sound cross too and to point to each word as they say it. The children may notice that the loudness of each word is indicated by the size and boldness of the print. As the bears get crosser so the print size grows. Children will then be alert for this device in other books too and will wait for you to respond in pitch to such words. This again encourages word spotting and recognition. Sometimes children think but don't ask questions like, 'I wonder where it says "help?"'. Because you shout it when you come to it, your children will soon make the link and recognise that word wherever they come across it.

If your children are fascinated by the thought and speech bubbles in *Teddy Bear's Moving Day* by Susanne Gretz, *What's that Noise?* by Mary Roennfeldt and *At the Beach* by Kerry Argent you could help your children to make their own books with thought and speech bubbles. Many of those 'awful' photos you've taken are great for this. Photos where the children are grimacing, yawning, crying, laughing and generally not looking their best can stimulate very funny thought and speech ideas.

I'm saying 'Get off my foot!'

The captions that your children suggest can be added to the photo as a speech bubble. Books like this not only make use of your worst photos but will also become favourite reading material with your children. And again because they reflect your children's language and convey their ideas they will be very readable.

'Noisy' books have great appeal for children too. Books like *Bertie and the Bear* invite children to join in with the various noises and as we all know only too well they will toot, toot, blah, blah and yip, yip with great enthusiasm. As you share books like these, the children are visibly awaiting the picture and voice cues that indicate it's their turn. Pause and point to the words leaving space for the children to join in.

Perhaps the best-known kind of joining-in books are these which use rhyme and repetition. Many of the traditional stories like 'The Gingerbread Man', 'The Three Billy Goats Gruff' and 'The Three Little Pigs' come into this category. Initially children will join in on the last word of each line or the rhym ing words and soon will be chanting the whole repetitions.

'By the hairs on my chinny chin chin,

I will not let you come in!'

Using books of this type can enable children to feel as though they are reading. They can confidently recall the story but also they know that they are using exactly the language of the book as they do so. Confidence stems from this and so does the children's perception of themselves as readers.

For example, *My Cat Likes to Hide in Boxes* uses both rhyme and repetition as the story unfolds. After reading the book several times to your children and talking about the pictures next time you read the book, pause at the end of each second rhyming line for the children to predict or recall the missing rhyming word.

'The cat from France liked to sing and _____.'

As the story builds up pause for your children to complete 'but my cat likes to hide in _____ ?' On each subsequent reading additional pauses can be introduced so that as well as using rhyme the children will now need to use recall and picture cues to help supply the missing words. If additional clues are needed give the first letter sound of the word,

'The cat from N _____ Got stuck in the doorway.'

Point at the word 'Norway' as this is going on, emphasising the visual clue N with the spoken one and then sliding the finger along. Don't labour this, you are not teaching, just providing clues as to how we read. Clues which your child may or may not be attending to. Another clue would be to say, sounds like doorway but begins with 'Nor...' In either case the children's knowledge of language and rhyme and in particular their feeling for the structure and language of this book will be helping them to find meaning in the book, another vital step to becoming a thoughtful and fluent reader. That is one who expects to make sense of what they read, understanding and awaiting the unfolding story rather then plodding on word by word.

Since beginning to read is basically a language skill we need to use books that also give children a chance to use their language skills. Picture books like, *The Gift* by John Porter provide opportunities for the children to use and demonstrate their understanding of stories, story structures and language styles. Some children will just pick up the books and begin telling the tale. For others though support is needed and questions will help. e.g.

'This book has no words in it. It's called *The Gift.*
'Who do you think the gift is for?'
'What do you think will be in it?'
'What are the children doing?'
'Do they like their chairs?'

Another technique is for you to begin the story leaving pauses for the children to continue if they want to. Whichever approach you or your children select, excitement and interest can be provided by you in terms of oohs, ah's, gasps, gulps or exclamations,

'Oh no, they're going into the sea!'

as the story is told or as comments and questions at the end.

'Did you know it would have a safe ending?'
'I loved your description of the underwater part!'
'So where did they visit, I've forgotten?'
'It was so scary in the jungle!'

Your children might like to make their story permanent by having parts written on 3M paper. These can be stuck onto the page without in anyway damaging the book, because they peel off easily when required.

As the children watch you write their captions they will be seeing and hearing how letters are strung together to make words.

writing > w-o-n-d-e-r i-f
speech > won der   if

They will begin to recognise some letters and some word shapes too and may even begin to use letters to represent words in their own pictures. And as you read their captions to them they will be confirming their early expectations about the permanence of writing — it always says the same thing everytime you read it.

I want to know about fossils.

Factual books require a different treatment both in terms of involving the children in the subject and in how they are read. For example a book on 'dogs' may have no initial appeal to your children but questions like, 'Do you think there's a dog like ours in this book?' 'I wonder which is the biggest type of dog?' may engage your children's curiosity. Factual books do not necessarily have to be read from cover to cover. You could decide to just look at the German Shepherd page. As you do this you can demonstrate new features of books and book conventions to your children. A table of contents, headings, pictures can be used to help find the way around a book. Skimming can be demonstrated, 'I wonder if it tells us what huskies eat. I'll just have a quick look.'
Questions that children ask can be quickly researched thus promoting further curiosity.

'Where else do they find fossils? Show me on a map.' Children's own interests can be pursued.

When reading factual books let your children set the pace, choose which sections interest them, ask questions that they want answers to. Make research and a quest for knowledge relevant to their needs and demands.

It is not easy to make factual books into great reading. You can however interject with exclamations of surprise ('Well I never knew that before.'); delight ('Isn't that interesting, we'll have to tell Uncle Colin about that.'); and insight ('We must make sure we always let insects go back to their own environment after we've kept them for a few hours.').

Reading to babies and toddlers may be more interactive with pauses to point out pictures or for baby to point to recognised objects and say the words they know. Expression, intonation and pleasure are just as vital now as they are when reading to older children. Babies need to learn more about language than vocabulary. They need to hear different tones, see different gestures and hear the rhythm and pattern of language so that they can begin to use it too. They will enjoy the noises in noisy books, the rhythm in rhyming books, the gentleness in bedtime books, the rumbustifications in riotous books just as much as older children do.

In summary, we see that children can benefit enormously from experiences with a variety of books. That beginner readers learn a lot from being read to, joining in with and making up their own stories. Children need experiences with the language of stories, with story structures, with rhyme and rhythm, with picture books to develop early understandings of what reading is and what is involved.
But remember:

o Reading should be enjoyable and fun.
o Children should be interested and curious about the books.
o Children should not be expected to join in if they don't want to.
o Feelings and emotions will be aroused by the books you share.
o This is a sharing process not a teaching process.

So:

o Read expressively and dramatically and encourage your children to join in with the same type of expression and drama.
o Help your child to engage with the book, its characters and storyline.
o Pause for your children to join in if they want to. Continue reading yourself if they don't want to.
o Let your children see that you are happy/sad/amused by the stories too.
o Provide the support and enthusiasm for reading so that your children will begin to think of themselves as readers and feel confident to have a go.

Activities

The activities in this section are for you on your own. They are suggestions that will help you to become a really good story teller. The more fluent, dramatic and expressive your reading is the more involved your children will be when you read, the more their attention will be held. In turn the more motivated they will be to want to read and the more fluent and expressive they will try to be when they read, or retell stories, so settle down in front of children's television and watch and attend to how professional storytellers tell stories. You can use the devices they use to bring stories to life,

- props to set the scene, a shawl or hat to make them look like a character from the book;

- eye movements and facial gestures;

- body language, sitting up tall for the giant, shrinking for the old woman;

- changes in voice, tempo, accent for each character;

- little asides to maintain interest.

Try some of these ideas out, make up some of your own. For example, you could:

- Try them in front of a mirror; listen to how you sound on tape.

- Read some of your children's books, get to know them well so that you can read them expressively, add props or costume, drama or gesture to them. Try reading *Crunch the Crocodile* with the assistance of your children's soft toys or toy animals. You are Crunch with snapping jaws, the animals are manipulated to run away, have a pow-wow.

- Make up some simple sound effect props so that next time you read a favourite story your children can be involved in adding sound effects to your rendition.

- Enlist your partner in the rehearsal of stories that you can read together.

CHAPTER 12

And Now for the Good News on TV

TV as an Anaesthetic

Some people think of television as a babysitter. I prefer to think of it as a drug — an anaesthetic. If rationed — and I do mean rationed, as overdoses build up an immunity — then television has a totally zonking effect on children. It's a miracle. Turning a bounding, rollicking, noisy ball of exuberance into a bug-eyed lump with the flick of a switch, is the sort of miracle that parents have wistfully dreamt about ever since Adam was a dad. Yet we parents who have this device at our finger tips, worry about it. We worry — rightfully — about the negative aspects of television. We worry about the violence. Though ironically, I have noticed children only become violent when you turn the damn thing off.

We parents worry about the drivel on television. How any human being can sit through the eighth re-run of Gilligan's Island astounds me. Is this what human kind has striven for over the eons? Is this why technologists have toiled to put satellites in fixed orbits and solar-powered receiving discs in remote locations? To saturate the world with repeats of Gilligan's Island?

We parents also worry about the sinister commercialisation of children's television timeslots. Television doesn't turn children into mini-consumers — no, they become MEGA-consumers and trade-name devotees. These children no longer sing, they jingle.

And so the average four year old doesn't want a packet of Smarties. They want a room full of Smarties with Cheezels hanging from the lights. Six-year-old boys want every sonic-blasting, hot-wheeled, super gizmo on the market, while six-year-old girls want a dainty little pastel-coloured cuddly Wuzzle which comes with 359 accessories (sold separately) and 93 other members of the Wuzzle family (collect the whole set). Eight-year-olds are more pragmatic. They want one thing — a little card emblazoned with the words American Express.

But of all the worries I grapple with regarding television, it is the assault on the mind that worries me most. No Disney or other cartoon, no mini-series, no film, no TV series has ever been as good as the original book. Good, but never AS good as the book. And how could they be? For a book is set on a stage as big as the universe, in a medium unrestrained by time or light or cost. A book has a cast of zillions with characters sweeter than the Spring air and more sinister than the deepest, dankest evil pit. For a book is set in your imagination. Your imagination can whisk you across a universe in an instant, take you for a ride on a dinosaur's back and seat you next to a president. Television can't do that.

So every so often — when it isn't the rating season — we switch the television off and turn on our imagination.

Come on Mum it's Play School.

You probably don't want to watch Play School or any of those other kids shows but there are many reasons why you should join your child and watch some television together. A sit down in front of the television can provide:

o a rest for you;
o a relaxed time for you and your children;
o something to share and talk about later;
o an extension to your children's experiences, in particular, their language experience;
o a stimulus for activities;
o a period of uninterrupted concentration.

Not only does television provide a relaxed and calm moment in the day it can also contribute to your children's development. If used carefully television can extend your children's background experiences and vocabulary. It can awaken curiosity and imagination, stimulate a hunger for more facts and information. Recall and comprehension can be aided too and even children with a short concentration span will sit and concentrate on their favourite show.

These claims are based on the premise that you do actually watch television with your children and that you select the programs to be watched fairly carefully. They also suppose that you make television interactive. You don't just sit quietly watching, saying nothing and then switch off and act as if nothing had just taken place.

Television is now a fact of life so let's make it earn its keep. Children come more easily to reading when they have had a broad language experience. This means not only that they have acquired a large vocabulary, but also and equally importantly that they have experienced language in a variety of forms. The books that you and your children have shared will have provided experiences of expressive language, descriptive language, rhyme and rhythm constructed by language. Television can add to this language experience.

'Let's cooperation.' said Richard
'Yes, if we cooperation we'll soon get this done.' replied Eddie.
'Look Mum, we're cooperationing.' said Richard.
'Oh, you are cooperating well, just as they were today on

Sesame Street' said Mum.

'Cooperating is fun' smiled Eddie.

This dialogue and action happened shortly after a Sesame Street show. Sesame Street had dealt with the topic of cooperation. Showing how, when three people share and cooperate they can all have what they want. From this brief cameo Richard and Edward had picked up a new word which they wanted to use. Also they were exploring the value and gains that cooperation brings with it. Mum was aware of what Sesame Street had shown that day so was able to appreciate the situation, relate it back to the television show, and also see the need to offer the verb, cooperate, to help them. Later that week the mother seeing the children squabble asked, 'Do you remember on Sesame Street the other day, how the children cooperated' With this prompt the children were able to recall the event, solve their difficulty, and have a good game.

So from a one minute sketch, the children had:

o learnt a new word;
o learnt something about cooperation;
o remembered and recalled and retold the sketch.

Remembering and recalling are an important part of learning to read. Children need to be encouraged and invited to recall and retell events. They love the opportunity to take the floor and talk too. But remember, television is not a baby minder. You need to be there to turn it into an active not a passive activity. If you are there, you can help your child interact with the program, you can help them to make links between past experiences, what they already know and what is being presented in the program they are currently watching. You can for example stimulate reflection by asking questions like,

'You saw one of those at the zoo, do you remember what it was called'

'Look that says Taronga Zoo. Is that the zoo we went to?' or by responding to your children's recollections,

'We saw an elephant didn't we mum?'

'Yes, and do you remember what the zoo keeper was doing?'

'He was scrubbing him'

You can then encourage your children to think about what might happen next by asking,

'What do you think the zoo keeper has in that bucket? What's he going to do?'

In this way you are encouraging your child to think and question as they watch. You can encourage them to think about and predict what might happen next and why. You can encourage your children to draw on their past experience and knowledge to compare what they already know with what they are being shown or told. This will help them comprehend more fully what they are watching. These same skills and understandings are required in the process of reading. Good comprehenders do these things naturally as they read.

His gadget umbrella won't work, I know it won't.

Even cartoon shows like Inspector Gadget can be used to develop comprehension skills, by asking questions like,

'Oh no, what is that Inspector Gadget going to do next?'

'Do you think they'll get out of the cave again, how?'

you are actually asking your children to use their knowledge of how stories develop to predict what might reasonably happen next. From their previous experiences of watching Inspector Gadget your children will know that one of his gadgets or his side-kicks will come to the rescue. They'll also know that Inspector Gadget always comes out on top. Written stories have these same types of conventions too. Children can use this story knowledge later to help them predict and comprehend stories they read themselves and stories that are read to them. They can also use it to help them to make up, tell and write stories of their own.

Cowboys live in the desert don't they Dad?

Some television programs are actually set or show places that you can never visit, the jungle, the Alps, the North Pole, a flood, the desert, the Grand Prix and so on. These settings are visual and aural. You can see in detail the flora and fauna of the jungle and hear the rain, the animals, the rustle of leaves and so on of the jungle. This information can be added to the storehouse in your children's brains so that when next you share a story set in the jungle their imagination has extra information, extra information to use to visualise and experience the setting.

Not only does the background experience gained from television broaden imagination, it also provides a range of experiences and general knowledge that can be used to help your children to interpret and comprehend books that would otherwise be outside their range of experiences.

Where do the stars go in the day time?

Some programs will leave your children asking questions.

'Do Kangaroos only have one baby at a time?'

'Why are dinosaurs extinct?'

Television can stimulate activity too. Activities arise from programs like Play School

'Can I have a tea party for my Ted?'

'Can we make orange jelly?'

Many of these activities will lead to reading, writing, reflecting on the program and use of the imagination, all vital to the reading process.

Some television shows and videos that can be hired are based on children's stories. These don't have to 'spoil' the children's books and in fact may enhance them. For example *How the Elephant Got His Trunk* can be a wonderful introduction to other stories by Kipling. The musical accompaniment adds to the children's imagination of the sounds of Africa. Comparisons between the illustrations on the video and in the book will lead to discussion about which most suit the story and why. The children can talk about or draw their interpretations. Conversation of this type develops critical thinking and requires deep comprehension of the story, its setting and its characters.

Play School wasn't as long today was it?

Television can help increase your children's concentration span. If you are sitting with your children you can help them to focus on the program being watched. During commercial breaks you can switch off the sound and talk about what's happened so far and what is still to come. Many children come to school unable to sit still and concentrate for more than twelve minutes, the usual amount of time between commercial breaks. Help your children sustain longer periods of concentration by interacting with them and encouraging them to interact with the show.

'Coka Cola, Cokealola is it.'

That's not to say that commercial breaks are to be banned. Children learn a lot from the ads. They begin to recognise signs and labels. They learn the jingles and they learn something about the society in which they live from the ads too. The message is don't overdo the ads and don't let them interrupt the concentration and interest in a good program. Make television work for you. Don't be slaves to it.

o Select carefully what you are going to watch.
o Switch the television off afterwards.
o Interact with the program, either as it goes along, or at the end as appropriate.
o Talk about what you've seen.
o Invite your children to retell or recount aspects of the program later.
o Select your programs together, carefully.

There can't be any hard and fast rules about how much television children should watch or how often. Some days there may be two consecutive programs that you would like to share. Other days there may be none. Of course a video could help here. The important thing is that television is seen as a special treat not as a constant backdrop to everything else. After all most programs of any worth will lead to further talk, curiosity, play activity or reading.

Activities

The first task really is to get to know what is on television that may be of interest to you and your children, or that might provide stimulus and broad experiences. That's not to say just pick out the educational ones. Choose programs that will lead somewhere.

- Look at the television guide and 'sample' a few programs.

- Watch a show with your children. Talk about it first 'I wonder what scrape Batman will get into today?' 'What dirty trick will The Penguin play?' Encourage them to predict subsequent events and to give reasons for their predictions. Retell it together afterwards, talk about the most exciting, best, worst bits.

- Watch and listen to your children as they watch television, follow up their questions or interests afterwards. Play School for instance usually suggests an activity, something to do or make as a follow up to the program. Your children may have expressed an interest in this so go off and do it.

- Choose a program of interest to the whole family such as a documentary on animals. Demonstrate your interest, discuss any issues, get out any related reference material or a map and follow it through. You may even have holiday snaps that relate to something shown. Involve your children in the 'excitement' or curiosity that the program generated.

And if you are too busy to watch a show with your children, turn the volume up a little so that you hear snatches of it. You can then follow up some aspects of it, ask questions related to it, expand ideas presented in it or repeat the rhymes or stories presented.

Television need not be the technological gadget that numbs the brain.

CHAPTER 13

The Cut and Pasters Weekly

──── Reading in the War Zone ────

Several years ago a cataclysmic event shattered my informed existence and ever since then I have struggled to maintain a sketchy view of the world news. You probably realise by now that several years ago I became a parent. Every week-day and once on a weekend since then a newspaper has been flung into my life. I know this because I get bills from this person called the newsagent. Yet in over seven years the only world news that seems to have filtered through to me is the fact that Prince Charles needs a hair transplant and that Imelda Marcos has size 5½ feet.

It wasn't so bad in the first year. I mean, there were not so many interruptions to my reading. But I was so tired I kept nodding off before I'd read the headlines. And I would wake up realising I had fallen asleep on a picture of Malcolm Fraser and dribbled over one of his best suits.

The toddler stage was worse. As soon as I sat down to read a newspaper, a little hand came up over the table, grabbed the paper, and took off scattering the sheets. I tried to reassemble the paper, but page 17 always ended up opposite page 33.

Then came the kinder stage. The kinder child would allow me to read. But the kinder child liked to lean on mummy. First I would read leaning to the left. Then I would read leaning to the right. Then the kinder child would climb up on my chair and lean forward like an affectionate Great Dane and I found myself once more trying to read with my nose buried in the newsprint.

School brought the age of the karate kid. No sooner would I sit down and open the newspaper than the headlines would leap towards me as a foot karate kicked the broadsheet. At this stage I couldn't rest the paper on the kitchen table as I also had a toddler intent on running off with the lot.

Now I read the paper folded into a small bundle, while standing in pyjamas fending off the toddler with one foot. This way I gather news in little bits. I know for instance that someone somewhere has declared war on someone else for some reason. In other words, nothing much has changed in seven years.

Yet all of these attempts to read a newspaper on the home front have taught my children something. It has taught them that newspapers are things you buy to recycle. And that's something.

'Snow White's on at 12.15, 2.15, and 4.15.'

There are items in the newspaper that you can share with your children. For example, if you are going on a picnic you can look at the weather forecast, if you want to watch television you can use the television guide. If your children were fascinated by the floods on television you can read them parts of the report in the paper. If you want to see a movie, buy a new car, you can use the paper. As you share the paper in this way your children could be learning about:

o newspaper reporting style;
o advertising style;
o the variety of information contained in the paper;
o new words, places and things;
o different layouts for different purposes.

Although this information has no real importance in the immediate life of your children it does have long-term importance. It is helping your children to build up expectations of print, an informal knowledge of the conventions of print. After looking at advertisements in the newspaper they will recognise the form of an advertisement, how it's set out, the language used, the purpose of it — information that will help them spot other advertisements and predict what's in them, information that is necessary to later reading and writing activity in school. Using the television guide develops knowledge of other conventions too: how a list is made, set out and sequenced, how the time can be shown in writing without a clock face. Some recognisable words will be present — words like Sesame Street, Play School, Inspector Gadget. Although sharing the television is not a teaching experience it is a learning experience. The conventions will be noticed and referred to in later reading experiences and if your children recognise some of the words they will feel like 'readers' and want to recognise more words and use the television guides again on other occasions.

'Why do people kill other people?'

Also as you share the paper, things will need explaining, clarifying in response to questions that your children ask:

'Where is Africa?'
'Why is she wearing that funny dress?'
'What's an election?'
Magazines with their coloured photographs are particularly interesting to children. Often they provide pictures of babies and toddlers, pets and familiar objects that children immediately associate with.

'Tell me about when I was a baby.'   Jane

Pictures can be the stimulus for talk, for stories, for questions and for reading and writing. Looking at a mother and baby special in a magazine really aroused Jane's interest. She wanted to know exactly what she was like as a baby, what she wore, what she ate, whether she messed in her nappy. She cut out pictures of babies and toddlers from the magazine and made a collage. She demanded captions to be written,
    'She's not got a nappy on,'
    'This one's pretty.'
She listened to stories about herself, she asked questions and wanted to see pictures of herself. These were then made into an album with some of the stories about Jane as a baby.

Babies and small toddlers respond well to pictures in magazines too. Objects can be pointed to and named. Similar objects in the home environment can be matched to the ones on the page. Names of objects can be expanded to include extra information and introduce new ideas and words.
    'Look there's a big tree with red flowers.'
    'The mummy dog's got some puppies. Little babies.'
    'The horse is neighing. Neigh! Neigh!'
Words and products that are familiar to the children from their own environment can be found in the advertisements,
    'Here's a Simpson cooker,' said Claire.
    'How did you know it's a Simpson?' asked Mum.
    'It says Simpson here, see, it's not our cooker is it Mum?'
    'No, it's different isn't it?'
    'Our dishwasher's a Simpson isn't it?'
Claire often asked what the words around the house said, but

Sandy (her Mum) didn't realise that Claire could actually read them and recognise them in different settings.

'I really only answer her when she asks, 'What does this say?' because I know I'll get no peace till I do answer her. It had never occurred to me that I was teaching her to read. I'll be a bit keener to answer her in future.'

Sandy might never have known, nor Claire have the opportunity to demonstrate this transfer of knowledge, if she and Sandy had not sat and flicked through the magazine together.

Children really enjoy seeing familiar household items in magazines. Apart from recognising the packet, label or brand name, they also get a sense of belonging. Children seem to derive security and comfort from knowing that there are other places and people just like theirs and them.

Does this say Roast Chicken?   Eddie

Sharing the glorious food pictures as you choose a recipe is something that children love to do. Together you can read the names of the ingredients using the information to make the decision as to what to cook or buy. There are two important reading skills involved in this type of activity. The first, extracting information from a list of factual text requires a different kind of reading from that required in fiction and stories. Similarly the second, following instructions, requires attention to detail and sequence where the outcome really can be affected if careful and accurate reading has not taken place. These are aspects of reading that can be discussed and demonstrated to your children as you cook.

'Now what do I do next. Oh yes, add the sugar. What would happen if I forgot the sugar?'

The 'craft', 'do-it-yourself' and 'gardening' sections also present instructions. Each has its own language style and special layout. By involving your children in a broad range of writing styles you are also broadening their understanding of and expectations of how print works. Magazines and newspapers contain a wide range of different print styles, layouts, writing styles and purposes for writing. Share some of these with your children. Read the letter from grandma telling a funny story about her grandchild, the doctor's column that says how you should treat an upset tummy, your stars for the month, the editors column or the list of contents. If it has a children's section make the most of that.

In summary, periodicals can provide stimulus for talk, for vocabulary extension, for using and trying new language styles and formats. They can arouse curiosity and stimulate interest. They can provide ideas for activity and follow up. They start from a setting that children are familiar with, and can associate the home and family and extend beyond this. They provide many different purposes for reading, to gain information, to answer questions, to provide entertainment, teach new skills, to broaden ones view of the world.

Activities

- Give your children old magazines to handle, flip through, cut up. Even babies can handle an old magazine without you having to worry that they'll tear the pages.

- Make up scrap books from the cut outs and encourage your children to make up captions that you can record for them.

- If your children are interested in letters, such as the initial of their name, they could be encouraged to look for objects in the magazines that begin with the same initial.

- Use the television guide to discuss and plan the days viewing.

- Go straight to the cartoons and share the 'joke' with your children.

- Look at the supermarket ads together to see what's on special or seasonal and make a shopping list.

- Look at the fashion page and talk about the ones you do/don't like.

- Read the headlines, relate them to the news on television if you've already seen it. If not compare the key stories with those shown on the news.

- Talk about the weather and see how the weather report

matched. Make your own predictions for tomorrow, compare with the paper's prediction and then tomorrow see who was closest.

- Look at the births column, read some out, talk about the names. Show your children what you put in the paper when they were born or when you got married.

- Look at the recipe, shop for its ingredients, cook it together following the instructions step by step.

- Use the children's pages and encourage your children to contribute.

- Look at the homes section/nature section/famous people section and follow your children's leads or questions.

- Cut out interesting pictures for a scrapbook.

- Look up places shown on a map or globe.

- Make up news stories about your family and events. Write them out, add headlines and photos or drawings. These could be real or imaginary and if your children are in them you can be sure they'll want them read or to read them time and again.

CHAPTER 14

Dear Library Computer, this Book is Late Because...

——— 'Have You Eaten Any Good Books Lately?' ———

I have this vision of a cartoon. One baby turns to the other and asks, 'Have you eaten any good books lately?'

Babies are like that. They eat books. They chew books. And eventually, they read them.

But while you have a little book-chewer in the family up to say a three-year-old book-chucker, a trip to the library can be a terrifying event. Babies may need books but the clear message parents get is that libraries don't need babies. I would love to stand at the front counter of my local library with toddler in arms and child hugging my knee, shouting, 'Excuse me. Where is the book on how to keep young children quiet in the library?'

Once I have solved the logistics of selecting books with one child who wants to destroy the shelving and throw books at innocent bystanders and another child who wants to take home 25 books — three of which are identical, but favourites — then I love the library. I want to look at pictures. Read. Borrow tapes. Flick through magazines. And that's just in the children's section. I wish I could annexe the whole library to my house.

Alternatively, I thought we could live in the library, but I don't think they'd have us. So I settle for lugging home some of the library every few weeks and hope the computer doesn't notice when we sneak the books back just a few weeks late.

'Mum, what's an earthquake? Why do they happen?'

Question, questions, some more urgent and pressing than others. Some just have to be answered, and where might you find the answer? At the local library. The children's sections of most libraries have plenty of current children's books. Fiction, factual, picture, pop-up books. Books that are displayed at the right level for little people to sort through and choose and each time they visit there are more and different books waiting. Many libraries also put on special programs for young children. There are story telling sessions as well as story reading sessions. And librarians are really interested in the art of the story teller. They use interesting devices to involve the children more closely with the story. 'Children often listen better to a story told by a puppet than by a person. They'll also respond to and talk back to a puppet,' one children's librarian told me. Sometimes a felt board is used with pictures that can be moved around, removed, added to as the story unfolds. Sometimes these story time sessions have related follow up activities too. Hearing stories read and stories told encourages children to begin making up their own stories.

'Children need to hear a story interpreted in a number of ways' another librarian stated, 'so that they know there are lots of ways to tell a story and it's okay to change it, to make it scarier, funnier, sadder than it was at first.' 'After all' she said, 'that's what writers do.'

Some libraries now run baby/parent story sessions, and some libraries will come out to run sessions with groups of parents and their children. These are often organised through the local Nursing Mothers', Childbirth Education Trust or Preschool Association.

'I want a book about dinosaurs.'

There are so many dinosaur books, where do you begin? Ask the children's librarian or a good children's bookseller for their recommendations. They will know which books are at an appropriate level, which ones appeal most to young children. Many libraries now print booklists to help parents choose appropriate books. One of the libraries I spoke to has the following lists available at the moment:

o books to read to your baby;
o humorous books for 2–5 year olds;
o rhyme and verse books 1–5 year olds;
o books with boy/girl characters;
o this year's best storybooks for 3–5 year olds.

Another librarian told me, 'I make a point of looking at the social side of books. I know just what to recommend to say, a child with a new baby in the family, a child about to start school, a timid child, a greedy child, and so on. All books, that is good books, also have hidden messages.'

Children's libraries are cosy, cheerful, decorative places to be. They are an Aladdin's Cave. They are free (as long as you don't lose, destroy or forget to take books back...for the computer).

Activity

The librarians that I spoke to all had messages for parents that they wanted to include too. So here are a few of them.

- Use your library in conjunction with a good children's bookshop. Your children need to own some books that they are free to handle and love.

- Put the library books on a shelf out of reach when you are not using them or supervising their use. Display your children's books at their level so they can have free access to them.

- Start reading to your children as soon as you can, the earlier the better. Good habits are born young.

- Tell stories to your children as well as reading to them. Make up stories that involve your children in them or stories about when they were young.

- Show your children that you respect and treasure books by covering their books to keep them clean and durable. Explain to them why you do it.

- Let your children see you sit and read sometimes. Why not choose yourself a book while you are at the library.

- Change the names of the characters in the books you read to your children's names. Make them feel part of the story. Help them become totally involved.

CHAPTER 15

School: Now the Pressure is On

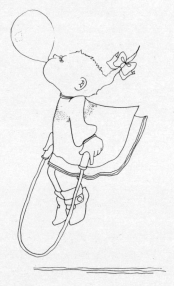

———— Please Take Care of My Little Genius ————

One wonderful aspect of the first two years in a child's life is that parents think their children are BRILLIANT. Babies don't have to do much to please parents. They just have to blow a few bubbles and roll over and their parents gasp 'Oh! Isn't she clever!' Or they stack three blocks and sing '1...2...3...' and daddy thinks 'We've got a bloody Einstein on our hands!'

Yes, for the first two years of a child's life the parents spend hours grinning at their little geniuses. And they are. They plop into the world as naked little blobs who spend the first three months of their lives gazing at their mothers from such an angle they must think they are being brought up by a pair of nostrils and a set of grinning teeth. Yet by four years of age these children can walk, talk, eat, grizzle, giggle and confound adults beyond belief. They are geniuses. And as long as parents take little notice of the rigid development guidelines set up by the experts their children remain geniuses until they reach school.

But the school start is the absolute end of every child's run as a genius. Kaput! THE END. There is a reason for this. It is not that the children aren't smart, it is that we parents — aided and abetted by teachers, other parents and assorted experts — suddenly redefine the word 'genius'. Once children hit the school community a genius is defined as one of those kids who can play the violin, has read the complete works of Enid Blyton, can classify dinosaurs, can calculate the national debt on their home computer, can name the member countries of the EEC and count to 939 in Roman numerals. And fair enough too.

But I am standing up for the many unsung geniuses of this world. Any child who can hop and gargle at the same time is a genius. Any child who can skip and chew gum is a genius. Any one who can hang upside down from monkey bars is a genius. (If you think it's easy, try it). Anyone who can do a cartwheel with a Vegemite sandwich in their mouth is a genius. Anyone who can write their name in sultanas is a genius.

There is no point trying to force a child to be more of a genius than they already are. Children learn at different rates. And as we have stressed in this book, all children are different. Don't forget, all geniuses are different too!

'I don't want to read to you now. I'm tired.'

If you haven't been into school since you were a child you may have quite a few surprises coming. Schools are not what they once were, formal rows of desks or tables always in one type of grouping.

You may find all kinds of different class arrangements, such as:

two classes sharing one classroom and two teachers working co-operatively; mixed ages in one class; parents in the classroom working with groups of children; children moving around using classroom resources or sharing their activity with other children/groups.

At any time in any day you might walk into a typical classroom and find many different seating arrangements, children sitting on the floor; in a circle; at a desk in front of the board (e.g. when learning letter formation); in the corridor.

You may not find a set reading scheme. You may not find flashcards (wordcards) or phonics (sounds) charts. You may find a negotiated curriculum where reading is related to current themes of special interest to the children or even initiated by them. Many of the books in the classroom will be related to the theme and will have come from the library.

You may find a completely different approach to when you learnt to read. You will find that children are encouraged to read, write and spell from day one. That is they are given books to read, books with strong picture clues so that the children can make up stories to match the pictures. Books that the teacher can plan themes around. Themes that have special interest to the children in the class.

You may find that individual children do not read to the teacher each day. That children do not work on one reading book until they are word perfect and then move onto the next book in the series. Instead you may find children as a class working on a big book with the teacher. Joining in on the parts they know. Matching words/sentences on strips (e.g. 'Little Miss Muffet sat on a tuffet?') to those in the text. You may find a group of children with small book versions of the big book, co-operatively reading and predicting the story. You may find children demonstrating their comprehension of a book by illustrating their favourite part or character, or by rewriting it changing characters or situations to create a new version of the story. You may find children reading their own writing to other children or the teacher.

The environment of the classroom is supportive of the children's first attempts to read, write and spell. Children are encouraged to think of themselves as readers and writers, even though early attempts may be 'parroting', 'scribbling' and almost incomprehensible. Teachers accept that just as babies learn to talk by babbling, refining the sounds they make, taking risks, trying out words and making up sentences that continually become closer to 'real language', so children will learn to read, write and spell, moving constantly closer to real reading, writing and spelling. In a supportive classroom the children will take risks, have a go. They will check their attempts, and in harmony with the teacher they will look at models of real writing and spelling. They will discuss patterns that they notice, regular and irregular spellings. They will extend their sight vocabulary (words they recognise) as they read, re-read and discuss the books they are reading. This approach is called a 'Whole Language Approach'. Language is used naturally. The children begin reading and writing in real and enjoyable situations. Real books, purposeful notices and captions, real writing, stories, letters, rhymes for others to read are the cornerstone of this approach. The process begins with meaning; only in the search for meaning are skills like letter or word recognition and sounds developed.

In summary then, expect:

o a friendly, stimulating and 'open' environment;
o parental involvement and participation to be welcomed and encouraged;
o a more child-centred approach (materials, books, themes chosen to reflect the children's interests);
o individual differences to be acknowledged and catered for (the activities resulting from reading allow the children to develop at their own pace);
o children to be encouraged to 'write' from day one (the same encouragement and responses offered in support of early writing and spelling attempts as were offered by you when your child was learning to talk);

o that early reading will not be word perfect (there will not be instant recall of isolated words);

o children to take risks as they read because, later, as they read for meaning, they will be able to guess at unknown words and begin to use first letter of the word to check their guess, e.g. the child reads 'lamb' but notices the s in 'sheep' and stops to have another go at the word;

o the emphasis to be on the process of reading/writing/spelling and not on the end product. (thinking, reasoning and trying to make sense are the key elements of effective reading and these are developed from day one in school);

o children to be inventing writing and spelling.

Activity

So how can you help? Schools value and respect the parents' desire to help their children and their need to understand and be part of the learning process. They do not see parents as interfering or meddling if they want to participate. In fact many schools recognise and advertise the fact that parents have a major role to play both in the children's development and in the classroom. Schools need parents to:

● work with groups of children;

● type up children's stories;

● help make class books;

● tell/read stories to the children...

and much more too. Some schools run sessions for parents to try to explain current theory and methods used. Schools want to involve you, so:

● stay in close touch with the school;

● talk to your child's teacher;

● become a parent helper;

● attend parent/teacher workshops;

- support the teacher (don't criticise or compare teachers in front of children);

- follow on the school's positive, supportive approach.

Some Misconceptions that Parents Hold

When I talked to teachers about advice they would like to give, teachers focused on misconceptions that some parents have, misconceptions that sometimes conflict with the child's needs or the schools approach.

Parent: My child is only in Grade 1 so it won't hurt to take him out of school for a three-week holiday.

Teacher: This is just not true. It probably matters more at this stage than any other, because during that period the rest of the class may make enormous progress. Some may become competent readers. Growth in the first year at school is fast and often spasmodic. After a three week break some children's competence and self confidence will have blossomed. The child returning to school may feel left out, left behind and suffer greatly in terms of confidence and self concept. He will perceive that he is not a reader. For some children this can be almost insurmountable.

Parent: Why doesn't my child bring set reading books or flash-cards home?

Teacher: For two main reasons. The first being that after a hard and busy day at school some children are just too exhausted for more teaching at home. The second being that we want children to share books with you, just as they share books at school. So books that we send home are meant to be read together. You read, pausing for your children to join in if and when they want to. Reading is seen as pleasurable not a task to be got through before TV can be switched on. Flashcards present words out of context. This is an inefficient way to learn words and scores low on motivation too. It is much more beneficial for your children to meet words in the meaningful context of a story, where their meaning can also be fully appreciated. Also since we are

109

encouraging children to take some responsibility for their own learning we encourage them to choose books that they want to read or have read. Motivation and interest are essential ingredients in the development of reading.

Parent: Why doesn't my child read to you everyday?

Teacher: There are two answers to this question. The first is that your child does read to me everyday. It's just that he/she is not standing beside me reading from the set book. All children work in groups to re-read, discuss or respond to books everyday. I visit all groups and listen to all the children. In addition to reading to/with me the children are also reading to/with each other, visitors to the classroom, and parent helpers. Compare the amount of and quantity of reading that your child is actually doing with what would happen if your child read to me for about one minute each day. In one minute we could say hello, find the page, read one page, work out one or two words. We could not feel positive towards books, feel warm and friendly and relaxed, spend time interpreting and comprehending what was read, discover the child's strengths and weaknesses, develop a program of development. Which would you prefer?

Parent: Why is my child often in a different reading group?

Teacher: Because in our classroom we do not have a top reading group and a bottom group. We accept that children are all individuals who develop at different rates. So we observe the children's reading behaviour and when several children seem ready to meet a new writing style, have a favourite author or story topic, ask the same questions, e.g. 'What are these marks for?', we plan a group session to cater for those particular needs, questions or interests. This is a child-centred, child-paced approach.

CHAPTER 16

But I Hate Reading

―――― How to Remain Almost Calm when Your ――――
―――――――― Child Refuses to Read ――――――――

There are two ways of looking at a child's refusal to read. There is the parent angle. This angle gains colour based on fear, terror, anxiety, bewilderment and frustration. Children must learn to read. They just must. And that's final. Then there is the child's angle. And it's simple.

'Yes, I do want to read. I do. But I'm very busy at the moment. I've got to run and jump and do things. And I would like to read. But would you honestly enjoy a book which goes 'Run...run. run. run...run.' They've given me, who knows all sorts of things about everything, they've given *me* a book like that! It's baby stuff. And it's boring. Better if they had given me a book called

'Vomit...vomit...vomit, vomit, vomit...'

'I want to read the big books. But they're too long. Too hard. Too many words. And I get cross with them. But I will learn to read...I'll learn tomorrow...Heh guys! Wait for me. I want to play too...'

And they are right. Who would want to read under those circumstances?

But if you keep reading to them, if they maintain an interest in books, magazines, toy catalogues, menus and graffiti, they will learn to read. Because they will see VALUE in reading and appreciate the POWER of the written word. After all, it is not the skill that counts, but the purpose. There are plenty of people shuffling around this country who can read, but only exercise this skill to differentiate between cans of SWAN LIGHT and FOSTERS LAGER. They have the skill but not the purpose. You can give your child a sense of purpose.

Now let me throw one more positive thought in your direction. If your children are dreamily ambling through childhood or bouncing their way through boyhood, half their luck. They are probably happy and in no hurry. It's only their parents who are getting anxious and want them to get on with it.

So what should you do? Make them miserable? After all many, many miserable children over the years — you may have known a few — were great readers. It was their escape. So what are you dealing with — happy realist rather than a miserable escapist? You should be delighted.

And despite any anxiety on your part I can pretty well guarantee — even in the most severe cases — that you will not be reading bedtime stories to your children when they are twenty-five-years-old. Think about it. Can you imagine them sitting up in bed saying,

'Please Mum, read me the BMW brochure tonight?' or 'Come on Dad, just read me the Avon catalogue one more time?'

I doubt it.

Of course, I could be wrong. But if you are still reading to your children twenty years from now, let me offer a word of advice. Get some Porsche brochures. Those BMW brochures are really boring.

'I don't want to read this book, it's boring.'

So, we've done our best. We've read to our children, talked to them, given them lots of different experiences and they go to school and don't become readers. We know, and the school knows, our children are bright enough, have a good vocabulary and general knowledge, but they don't know why our children are not reading better. The question of blame arises.

'Why doesn't the school...?'

'If only I'd done...?'

'Why don't children listen and concentrate these days?' Questions that sap the energy. Energy that could be spent working on the problem, designing and trying out strategies to help.

There are two types of 'non' readers. Those for whom reading for some reason is hard and those for whom reading is not hard but the motivation to want to read is lacking, children who can read but don't want to. In either case the children may develop a lack of confidence in themselves as readers and as people. The sense of failure may exert pressure on them to achieve. Pressure that prevents them from achieving. When you know you can't do something, you think that something is hard, that you'll never be able to do it. Attitudes develop that make reading even harder and more unattainable.

There is a lot that parents can do to help children who do not read. So much in fact that it could fill another book. The basic messages though, are still the same as the ones presented in this book:

o Reading is 50% motivation.
o Children must be enticed into reading.
o Reading must be pressure free.
o Reading must be seen as fun, entertaining and purposeful.

Motivation must be kept alive. As long as your children are motivated to want to read they will continue trying. Motivation can be aroused and maintained in a number of ways. Books that interest your children can be a source of motivation. Look for books that relate to your children's interest. Look for books that contain fascinating stories written in a simple style yet with some literary merit. Try a whole range of different types of books, joke books, riddle books, story books, do-it-yourself books, factual books, comic books. If your children want to read it you are half way there. If your children bring 'dull' books home from school to read, help them get through them quickly and painlessly and then read them something that they like. A spoonful of sugar may help the medicine go down.

Always quit while you are ahead. If the reading is going well, stop before it becomes a chore. Leave the children feeling 'that was good' and tell them they did well, praise them, give their confidence and motivation a boost.

By choosing books that appeal to your children and keeping the experience fun, you will be enticing your children into books and into wanting to read. Put all you've got into the stories so that the full impact and pleasure of a book can be savoured, a further enticement. Try to take the pressure off your children. Rather than ask them to read to you, read to them and invite them to join in. For example, you could read the main part of the story and invite your children to be Jack or the giant. By sharing the reading task in this way your children will feel like readers. They will be participating fully in the reading, following the words closely as you read and then reading just the few words that Jack says. They'll have all of the pleasure and none of the pain.

Tape some stories, ones that your children really love, so that they can sit and listen to them and follow them in the book when they are in the mood. Encourage them to join in with their favourite parts.

Make it a rule to read a book or passage to your children at least once before you ask them to read it to you. In this way any unfamiliar or hard words can be anticipated and tackled by your children. Also in doing this you will be presenting a model of fluent and expressive reading for your children to emulate when they read the book themselves. Never ask your children to read out loud to you until you have either read the book to them or they have discussed the title and possible story content and quietly rehearsed the book first. For example you can ask, 'That looks like an interesting book, what's it called?' 'Who's in it?' 'What's the story about?' quite naturally and spontaneously when a book is brought home from school. You can then say, 'I'll just finish this job. You look at the book, see if there's any words you don't know and then I'll come and help you and we'll read it together.'

Hopefully, interest will be aroused, the pressure will be off and the two of you can have a cosy, friendly read and chat.

Resist that temptation to push and prod and teach. Let your children set the pace, respond positively;

'Wow! I didn't know you could read long words like 'dinosaur' rather than,

'That doesn't say 'when' it says 'went"

Remind yourself every now and then how you supported your children when they were learning to talk, offer them the same support now that they are learning to read.

Of course, if after a short time you are still worried about your children's progress, discuss it with the school who will be able to diagnose any particular problems that may require more specialist help.

Appendix

The books listed in this Appendix are not the only ones available, rather they reflect the ones that we have used and know to be popular with children. You may have others already in your children's library that would be equally suitable. Also your local library may be very supportive and helpful in providing appropriate books.

Most of the books listed here are in fact story books of very high quality. However, we have categorised them as Story Books, Picture Books and Joining-in Books, to help you see how they can be used and how your children might respond to them. This list is meant as a guide, not a definitive list. If you are just beginning your children's library the list will provide some starters and some standards by which to compare other books.

BOOKS FOR BABIES AND TODDLERS

Board Books
Pets *Valerie Greely* Blackie
Little Numbers *Rodney Peppe* Methuen
Good Morning *Dick Bruna* Methuen
Baby's First Book Ladybird
Talk about Animals Ladybird
Talk about House Ladybird
Talk about Shopping Ladybird
Nursery Rhyme Books Ladybird
1,2 and 3 Bedtime Rhymes Ladybird

Spot Books
Spot's First Walk *Eric Hill* Puffin
Where's Spot *Eric Hill* Puffin
Spot's Birthday Party *Eric Hill* Puffin
Spot's First Christmas *Eric Hill* Heinemann

Noisy Books
Bertie and the Bear   *Pamela Allen*   Puffin
I Can Roar   *Frank Asch*   Angus and Robertson
See Mouse Run   *Sally Grindley and Priscilla Lamont*
   Hamish Hamilton
Goodnight Owl   *Pat Hutchins*   Puffin

OLD TIME FAVOURITES

The Tale of Peter Rabbit   *Beatrix Potter*   Frederick Warne
The Little Engine that Could   *retold by Watty Piper*   Collins
Little Tim and the Brave Sea Captain   *Edward Ardizzone*   Puffin
Harry the Dirty Dog   *Gene Zion*   Puffin
Harry By the Sea   *Gene Zion*   Puffin
Mike Mulligan and his Steam Shovel   *Virginia Le Burton*   Puffin
The Story About Ping   *Marjorie Flack*   Puffin
The Story of Babar, The Little Elephant   *Jean de Brunhoff*
   Methuen
Winnie the Pooh Stories   *A.A. Milne*   Methuen

MODERN CLASSICS

Mog the Forgetful Cat   *Judith Kerr*   Picture Lion
Mog's Christmas   *Judith Kerr*   Picture Lion
Frog and Toad All Year Round   *Arnold Lobel*   Scholastic
The Bad Tempered Ladybird   *Eric Carle*   Puffin
Possum Magic   *Mem Fox*   Omnibus
The Balloon Tree   *Phoebe Gilman*   Scholastic
Alexander and the Terrible, Horrible No Good, Very Bad Day
   Judith Viorst   Blue Gum
The Tiger Who Came to Tea   *Judith Kerr*   Puffin
Whistle Up the Chimney   *Nan Hunt*   Collins
Hemi's Pet   *Joan de Hamel*   Angus & Robertson
Boy Was I Mad!   *Kathryn Hitte*   Puffin
Don't Forget the Bacon   *Pat Hutchins*   Puffin
Mr Gumpy's Outing   *John Burningham*   Puffin
There's a Sea in My Bedroom   *Margaret Wild*   Puffin
Can't Catch Me   *John Prater*   Puffin

FOLK TALES AND FAIRY STORIES

A Piece of Straw   *Junko Morimoto*   Methuen
The Puffin Children's Treasury   Viking Kestrel

The Fairy Tale Treasury   *Raymond Briggs*   Puffin
Tikki Tikki Tembo   *retold by Arlene Mosel*   Scholastic
Richard Scarry's Animal Nursery Tales   *Richard Scarry*
  Golden Press

JOINING-IN BOOKS

Goodnight Owl   *Pat Hutchins*   Puffin
Mister Magnolia   *Quentin Blake*   Collins
In the Middle of the Night   *Amanda Graham*   Era
Nicky's Noisy Night   *Harriet Ziefert*   Puffin
The Gingerbread Man   *Traditional*   Various editions
The Enormous Turnip   *Traditional*   Various editions
The Fat Cat   *Jack Dent*   Puffin
Hattie and the Fox   *Mem Fox*   Ashton Scholastic
Monster Can't Sleep   *Virginia Meuller*   Puffin
A Playhouse for Monster   *Virginia Meuller*   Puffin
Bertie and the Bear   *Pamela Allen*   Puffin
Mr McGee   *Pamela Allen*   Puffin
Hairy Maclary From Donaldson's Dairy   *Lynley Dodd*   Puffin
Knock, Knock, Who's There?   *Sally Grindley*   Magnet
Teddy Bear's Moving Day   *Susanna Gretz*   Collins Lion
At the Beach   *Kerry Argent*   Omnibus
What's that Noise?   *Mary Roennfeldt*   Puffin
The Three Billy Goats Gruff   *illustrated by Graham Percy*   Hamlyn
The Three Little Pigs   *Traditional*   various editions
My Cat Likes to Hide in Boxes   *Eve Sutton*   Puffin
Have You Seen My Duckling?   *Nancy Tafuri*   Puffin
Across the Stream   *Mirra Ginsburg*   Puffin
Wake Up Bear   *Lynley Dodd*   Puffin
1 Hunter   *Pat Hutchins*   Puffin
Hairy Maclary's Bone   *Lynley Dodd*   Puffin
Each Peach Pear Plum   *Janel & Allen Ahlberg*   Puffin
The Very Hungry Caterpillar   *Eric Carle*   Puffin
This is the Bear   *Sarah Hayes*   Walker
One Duck, Another Duck   *Jose Aruego*   Julia MacRae
Jump Frog Jump   *Robert Kalan*   Julia MacRae
Who Sank the Boat?   *Pamela Allen*   Puffin

TELL IT YOURSELF STORY BOOKS

The Snow Man   *Raymond Briggs*   Hamish Hamilton
The Gift   *John Prater*   Puffin
Rosie's Walk   *Pat Hutchins*   Puffin
Doing the Washing   *Sarah Garland*   Puffin
Moonlight   *Jan Omerod*   Puffin
On Friday Something Funny Happened   *John Prater*   Puffin

FAR AWAY TIMES AND DISTANT LANDS

A Pet for Mrs Arbuckle   *Gwenda Smyth & Ann James*   Puffin
Have You Seen My Cat?   *Eric Carle*   Picture Knight
The Knight and the Dragon   *Toni De Paola*   Methuen
I've Got a Secret   *Betty Evans*   McGregor
The Shy Dragon   *Marie Jose Sacre & Jindra Strnad*   Methuen
I'm Going on a Dragon Hunt   *Maurice Jones*   Puffin
There's a Dinosaur in the Garden   *Michael Salmon*   Lamont
Long Neck and Thunderfoot   *Helen Piers*   Puffin
The Snowy Day   *Ezra Jack Keats*   The Bodley Head
Teddy Bears Take the Train   *Susanna Gretz & Alison Sage*   Hippo
The Proud and Fearless Lion   *Ann & Reg Cartwright*   Beaver

BOOKS FOR THE IMAGINATION

The Mixed Up Chameleon   *Eric Carle*   Puffin
In the Night Kitchen   *Maurice Sendak*   Puffin
Would You Rather Be a Bullfrog?   *Theo Le Seig*   Collins
One Dragon's Dream   *Peter Pavey*   Puffin
Wombat Stew   *Marcia K. Vaughan*   Ashton Scholastic
Tom and Sam   *Pat Hutchins*   Puffin
Changes Changes   *Pat Hutchins*   Puffin
Arthur   *Amanda Graham & Donna Gynell*   Methuen

ALPHABET BOOKS

Alphabet   *Fiona Praghoff*   Gollancz
Dr Seuss's ABC   Collins
Richard Scarry's ABC Word Book   *Richard Scarry*   Collins
Ant and Bee and the ABC   *Angela Banner*   Kaye and Ward
Animal Capers   *Kenny Argent*   Omnibus
Teddy Bears ABC   *Susanna Gretz*   Collins Lion
A is for Australia   *John Brennan*   Dent

John Burningham's ABC   *John Burningham*   Cape
ABC   *Brian Wildsmith*   Oxford University Press
ABC   *Elizabeth Cleaver*   Oxford University Press

FACTUAL BOOKS

Baby Animals   *photographed by Kathie Atkinson*   Allen & Unwin
Ant Cities   *Arthur Dorros*   Crowell
One Hungry Spider   *Jeannie Baker*   Ashton Scholastic
Building a House   *Byron Barton*   Collins
Animal Pictures   *William Stobbs*   Bodley Head